"Skillfully tracing the intertext between artistic illuminations and biblical passages, Jonathan Homrighausen's sensitive exegeses afford exquisite depth and dimension to three familiar biblical traditions as well as invite readers to experience for themselves *The Saint John's Bible*. Tracing the motif of trees across Jesus Family Tree in Matthew's Gospel, the Trees of Knowledge and Life in Women's Biblical Stories, and the centrality of Trees in the Creation Traditions, Homrighausen ignites our imagination with new possibilities not only for fresh interpretations of these texts but also for how they urgently summon us to the promotion of justice."

—Gina Hens-Piazza
    Professor of Biblical Studies, Joseph C. Alemany Endowed Chair
    Jesuit School of Theology of Santa Clara University

"Jonathan Homrighausen has done what the creators of *The Saint John's Bible* hoped for most. He has explored its 'beautiful persuasion' to reveal the way its beauty speaks across volumes and across audiences as it proclaims the Good News. *Illuminating Justice* is truly a joy to read. While going deep into key images in *The Saint John's Bible*, Homrighausen shows how this Bible, while using ancient tools and traditional materials, fits into a new world of theological thought. It is one that approaches the relationship between Catholics and Jews, the role of women, and creation care, in fresh and empowering ways. This volume rings with insight and draws our attention to the work of numerous contemporary theologians and artists. Reading it, one will discover things not just about art, but also about living out one's faith in the 21st century."

—Susan Sink
    Author of *The Art of* The Saint John's Bible: *The Complete Reader's Guide*

"'Beauty is in the eye of the beholder,' a phrase coined in the nineteenth century by Margaret Wolfe Hungerford, corresponds with what today's biblical interpreters refer to as 'the world in front of the text.' In other words, there is a subjective quality to all interpretation. Jonathan Homrighausen here provides us with a stunning example of such interpretation. Reading the exquisite illuminations found in *The Saint John's Bible*, he lifts up three ethical-sacramental themes: respect for Jewish sensitivities; attention to feminist concerns; and appreciation for natural creation. In this remarkable book, he thus shows us that art is not only an expression of beauty, but of justice as well."

—Dianne Bergant, CSA
    Professor Emerita of Old Testament Studies
    Catholic Theological Union

ILLUMINATING JUSTICE

The Ethical Imagination
of *The Saint John's Bible*

JONATHAN HOMRIGHAUSEN

FOREWORD BY MICHAEL PATELLA

LITURGICAL PRESS
Collegeville, Minnesota

www.litpress.org

1   2   3   4   5   6   7   8   9

Library of Congress Cataloging-in-Publication Data

Names: Homrighausen, Jonathan, author.
Title: Illuminating justice : the ethical imagination of the Saint John's Bible / Jonathan Homrighausen.
Description: Collegeville, Minnesota : Liturgical Press, 2018. | Includes bibliographical references and index.
Identifiers: LCCN 2017055814 (print) | LCCN 2018022319 (ebook) | ISBN 9780814644799 (ebook) | ISBN 9780814644553
Subjects: LCSH: Bible—Criticism, interpretation, etc. | Social justice—Biblical teaching. | Saint John's Bible—Illustrations. | Social justice in art.
Classification: LCC BS680.J8 (ebook) | LCC BS680.J8 H66 2018 (print) | DDC 220.5/20434—dc23
LC record available at https://lccn.loc.gov/2017055814

To Michelle Runyon

and

All whose hearts and minds are touched by
The Saint John's Bible,
especially those at Santa Clara University and
the Diocese of St. Augustine, Florida

CONTENTS

FOREWORD

Michael Patella

During solemn evening prayer on June 11, 2011, with the monks and the National Catholic Youth Choir singing Donald Busarow's majestic *Te Deum*, Donald and Mabel Jackson processed down the central aisle of Saint John's Abbey and University Church with the last page of the book of Revelation. They set it upon the altar for Abbot John Klassen and university president Father Bob Koopmann to emboss the gold leaf on the final word, *Amen.* Much had transpired from the time in 1996 when university president Brother Dietrich Reinhart, seeking counsel on the new venture, first gathered the theologians from the Saint John's School of Theology and Seminary. While one might consider the project completed with the ceremony on that June night, the real hope was that the celebration would signal a beginning.

Initially, the idea was to do something grand, not simply to write a Bible by hand and to include some good artwork. The monks, faculty, and administrators thought that if handwriting the Bible were worth anything, it would have to do more than become an interesting project destined to sit on a shelf. Rather, it would have to address issues of the day, incorporate the culture, include the broad spectrum of the humanities, explore science, be conversant with music, art, and literature, raise questions of justice, speak to other faith traditions, and be hospitable to other people of goodwill. In a word, in order to be a successful endeavor, it would have to reflect the glory of God and the Christian mission at this point in the history of the world.

To raise the project to such a level, Brother Dietrich formed the Bible Task Force whose charge was to develop a plan that would not only see the completion of *The Saint John's Bible* but one that would also ensure its influence on both Christian and non-Christian cultures once the ink was dry on the parchment. The Task Force settled, therefore, on six goals: ignite the imagination, glorify God's word, revive tradition, discover history, foster the arts, and give voice to the voiceless. Finally, the Task Force established the Committee on Illumination and Text, or CIT, to provide the theological input for the artists and to make the final decision on the images.

Following suit, the CIT employed these six objectives both in the initial schema or outline as well as in the resulting theological briefs written for each of the Bible's seven volumes. Above all, the Task Force intended that these goals continue well beyond the completion of the Bible. At no point, thought the Task Force, should anyone consider *The Saint John's Bible* to be an end in itself.

During the fifteen years that the artists and scholars worked on *The Saint John's Bible* and continuing shortly after, books and articles contemporaneous with the writing of the tome commented on and explained the production, calligraphy, and illuminations. Jonathan Homrighausen's *Illuminating Justice: The Ethical Imagination of The Saint John's Bible*, however, represents the first generation of commentary outside the production phase of the Bible. Moreover, *Illuminating Justice*, as the first work to respond to the mission of the Bible project, is also in the unique position of probing the completed Bible from the perspective of an interested scholar outside those who produced it.

In opening this book and studying the chapters, readers should bring their own experiences of Sacred Scripture to the text and images, and they should let these experiences begin a dialogue with the word of God. Jonathan Homrighausen did so, and the practice yielded the work you have before you. To do the same with these images, indeed with all images in *The Saint John's Bible*, is to invite the Holy Spirit into the conversation so that the insight of twenty-five hundred years of the biblical tradition can grow and flourish in this millennium and beyond.

ACKNOWLEDGMENTS

I t takes a village to write a book. In the case of *The Saint John's Bible*, that village was peopled by Donald and Mabel Jackson, the team of scribes and illuminators, the Committee on Illumination and Text headed by Michael Patella, the monks of Saint John's Abbey, and the many administrators behind the scenes who coordinated plane flights, held fundraisers so the project could see the light of day, publicized it to the world, created and sold Heritage Editions and trade editions, and performed myriad tasks needed for this Bible to come into the world and reach hearts and minds. Thankfully, my book was *far* less complex to create. But I still owe my village a great debt.

When I first approached Hans Christoffersen of Liturgical Press to pitch a book idea on *The Saint John's Bible*, I assumed I was one of many. To my surprise, he told me there was nothing in the pipeline in this area and was incredibly receptive to and excited by my ideas. My thanks to Hans for going to bat for this book and for trusting a younger writer.

Before working with *The Saint John's Bible*, I had little background in art history and had never heard of the work on art and the Bible done by reception history and visual exegesis scholars. Along the journey of this project, I am particularly indebted to Kathleen Maxwell for her tutelage in the world of manuscript studies and illuminated Bibles. Thanks also to Andrea Sheaffer's help on understanding visual exegesis, and the late Fr. Michael Morris's instruction in Christian iconography. Also, my understanding of the technique—and the difficulty!—of calligraphy would be very limited were it not for Sara Loesch-Frank.

Many people gave special input for particular chapters. I first tested out my material on Jewish-Christian dialogue at the Midwest Conference on Christianity and Literature, on a travel grant from the Center for Arts, Religion, and Education at the Graduate Theological Union, which later hosted my brown bag lunch lecture on the same topic. Leah Machinskas-Le gave me valuable insight for this chapter, particularly on the *Suffering Servant* illumination, as did Andrea Pappas. Diana Gibson, Justin Staller, and several members of the Catholic Biblical Association shared their insights for my material on feminist biblical interpretation. A special thanks to Glynis Mary McManamon, Caroline Mackenzie, and Joshua Koffman for allowing me to use images of their art.

Two people deserve special praise. Kitty Murphy was my first guru into the world of academic biblical scholarship and a model of how to be a scholar grounded in the academy but in service to, and in the tradition of, a believing community. David Pleins brought me on as coauthor for my first book and mentored me through the process of publishing this second book.

My fellow enthusiasts and experts in *The Saint John's Bible* likewise encouraged me at every step. Michael Patella, the chair of the Committee on Illumination and Text, encouraged me to dig deeper into this project, assured me that I was on the right track, and gave feedback on the entire book. Jason Paul Engel, OblSB, and Anne Kaese, ambassadors for *The Saint John's Bible* who have shown it to thousands of people over many years, shared with me their stories of how this project has touched the hearts and minds of their audiences. Larry Fraher, who has incorporated *The Saint John's Bible* into his recent dissertation (congratulations!) in Art and Religion at the Graduate Theological Union, shared with me some of his analyses of the illuminations. Susan Sink, whose book brims with insight into the illuminations, also answered a crucial question about the symbolism of the double-arched cathedral doorway. Thomas Ingmire and Suzanne Moore hosted me in their studios, regaling me with their stories behind each of their illuminations and filling in some details on what it was like to work with Jackson and the Committee. Conversations with Susan Wood, SCL, Irene Nowell, OSB, and Suzanne Moore also gave crucial insights. Special thanks to those who read all or part of the book draft: April Flowers, Michelle Runyon, David Pleins, Lucinda Mosher, Paul Crowley, SJ, Jason Paul Engel, OblSB, and Larry Fraher.

As *The Saint John's Bible* has consumed me for the last two years, I have been helped along the way in expertise and encouragement by fellow enthusiasts and teachers in two communities. I got my start on this work at the invitation of Sheila Conway of Santa Clara University Archives & Special Collections, who first tasked me with promoting the university's Heritage Edition. Sheila has been a constant dialogue partner and valuable skeptic. In writing a book, I suspect I went slightly beyond her expectations. My deepest appreciation also to the faculty of Santa Clara University and the Graduate Theological Union who let me test ideas for this book on their classes, including Kitty Murphy, Gary Macy, Diana Gibson, John Endres, SJ,

David Pleins, Jan Giddings, and Paul Crowley, SJ. Their students' questions and comments gave me many insights.

Once I had the contract for this book in hand and an outline of each chapter, I received an opportunity out of the blue from the Roman Catholic Diocese of St. Augustine, Florida, to teach a week-long intensive course on *The Saint John's Bible* for their Summer School of Theology. I organized the course around this book and was rewarded with an abundantly insightful and excited group of students. My deepest gratitude to everyone in the course, and especially to Erin McGeever, the diocese's Director of Formation, for extending me the opportunity and showing me the ecclesial sights of the diocese for the week.

Because this book emerges out of my teaching at Santa Clara and St. Augustine, I dedicate this book to all those in those communities whose lives are touched by *The Saint John's Bible*. As always, I am forever indebted to Michelle Runyon for her support, patience, and continual encouragement to follow my passion and write this book. Michelle, may I reciprocate as well when the time comes for you to write *your* first book!

All images from *The Saint John's Bible*, Copyright 2002–2011, Saint John's University, Collegeville, Minnesota, USA. Used by permission. All rights reserved.

Synagoga and Ecclesia in Our Time by Joshua Koffman, photograph taken by Joshua Koffman. Used by permission.

The Creator by Caroline Mackenzie, photograph taken by Caroline Mackenzie. Used by permission.

Protectress of the Poor by Glynis Mary McManamon, photograph taken by Glynis Mary McManamon. Used by permission.

Excerpts from documents of the Second Vatican Council are from *Vatican Council II: Constitutions, Decrees, Declarations; The Basic Sixteen Documents*, edited by Austin Flannery, OP, © 1996. Used with permission of Liturgical Press, Collegeville, Minnesota.

All Scripture quotations from New Revised Standard Version Bible, © 1989 National Council of the Churches of Christ in the United States of America. Used by permission. All rights reserved worldwide.

PREFACE

The continuous process of remaining open and accepting of what may reveal itself through hand and heart on a crafted page is the closest I have ever come to God. Now, I am led to the making of the Bible as a celebration of the Word of God for the twenty-first century in modern scripts, and I realize now it is the thing I have been preparing for all my life.[1]

—Donald Jackson, 2002

What am I doing, who is not a practicing Christian, not any affiliate to any major religion, with this job, with this Bible? Well, what I think I am doing is bringing an open mind. And what I am bringing is a . . . Christian cultural background, Western European, but also I'm seeing, in these ancient texts, totally relevant, instantly recognizable things which are going on around us.[2]

—Donald Jackson, 2012

Audacious as it sounds, it seems safe to declare *The Saint John's Bible* the most amazing Bible of the third Christian millennium. From the first illumination of the genealogy in Matthew, to the writing of the final "Amen," to its dissemination in galleries, Heritage Editions, and trade editions, people of all religions and walks of life are stunned by the beauty of this Bible.

What makes this Bible so appealing? For the last three years, I have presented the Heritage Edition of *The Saint John's Bible* to hundreds of people, from college students to professional calligraphers to church groups to scholars. I have shown this Bible to secular undergraduates in introductory

1. Donald Jackson, "The Dream and the Realities," *The Scribe: Journal of the Society of Scribes and Illuminators* 75 (Summer 2002): 3.

2. Donald Jackson, "Donald Jackson, Calligrapher" (lecture, EG Conference, Monterey, CA, April 12, 2012), https://vimeo.com/74350010.

Scripture courses with no exposure to the Bible, and I have shown it to members of the Catholic Biblical Association who have spent decades teaching and writing about Scripture. The effect is the same. This Bible succeeds as a work of art *and* a work of exegesis primarily because of its *beauty*.

The Saint John's Bible is not just a work of art, however. This unique Bible functions as a work of Catholic *biblical interpretation* in visual form. By repeating visual motifs throughout its illuminations, this Bible creates connections between different parts of the canon and the issues of our own time—as if *The Saint John's Bible* is a living, breathing entity creating "canonical conversations." This book traces three canonical conversations on social justice in *The Saint John's Bible*: a conversation on right relationship with Jews and Judaism; another on biblical women and feminist biblical interpretation; and finally, one on creation care. By focusing on these three conversations around contemporary ethical issues, we will see how *The Saint John's Bible* invites its viewer-readers to bring their own ethical-sacramental imagination to bear on both Scripture and the world.

The symbolism of trees serves as a unifying thread throughout the three conversations. In the first chapter, we look at the first illumination of *The Saint John's Bible*, the menorah frontispiece to Matthew that is Jesus' family tree, and Paul's image of the olive tree to describe the relationship between Jews and Christians. The chapter on women and Woman Wisdom begins with the Tree of Knowledge and ends with the Tree of Life. And for creation care, we see how every living tree is a tree of life from God. There is irony here: unlike most Bibles, *The Saint John's Bible* is not printed on tree products, but written on vellum. The tree also represents stability, longevity, and the deep-rootedness of tradition, both hallmarks of *The Saint John's Bible* and the Benedictine tradition that produced it.

One of the goals of *The Saint John's Bible* is to "ignite the imagination," not just of its creators, but of its viewers.[3] Just as the creators of *The Saint John's Bible* used their imaginations to make magnificent art, so I invite you to use your imagination as you approach *The Saint John's Bible* and your own spiritual life. I hope this book spurs not only deeper exegesis, but also personal transformation.

As I write this book, I have in mind the many different audiences to whom I have had the pleasure of introducing *The Saint John's Bible*, from professional calligraphers interested in its technique and scripts to biblical scholars focused on its exegesis. While I discuss this Bible with the depth

---

3. Michael Patella, *Word and Image: The Hermeneutics of* The Saint John's Bible (Collegeville, MN: Liturgical Press, 2013), xi.

and nuance of a Scripture scholar, apart from the terms introduced in the first chapter I try to avoid technical jargon. I especially offer this book to ministers and preachers who wish to bring this remarkable Bible to their congregations, to the librarians and curators charged with showing the Heritage Edition in academic and museum contexts, and to undergraduate faculty who wish to bring *The Saint John's Bible* into courses on Scripture and theology.

This book in no way replaces the excellent works by Michael Patella, Susan Sink, and Christopher Calderhead, but merely offers a different window through which to look at *The Saint John's Bible*. Sink and Patella unpack individual illuminations, comprehensively surveying the whole project; however, they do not systematically survey the repeated symbolism of this Bible and its conversations between different parts of Scripture and contemporary Catholic biblical interpretation. Unlike them, I do not survey every illumination, only those which fit the themes of this book. Hence this book supplements, not replaces, previous works on this Bible. Nor do I pretend that mine is the last word!

At the start of *The Saint John's Bible* project, the Committee on Illumination and Text formulated three key themes that this Bible was to stress: hospitality, conversion of life, and justice for God's people. I hope that by the end of this book you will better understand some of the specific ways in which this Bible calls us to live these virtues. Just as *The Saint John's Bible* illuminates the Word, may this book illuminate those illuminations.

Chapter One

BEAUTIFUL PERSUASION AND THE ETHICAL IMAGINATION

I n every facet of *The Saint John's Bible*, even down to the script Jackson devised for it, Jackson and the Committee on Illumination and Text overseeing *The Saint John's Bible* sought to reclaim the past while still making something fresh for the twenty-first century.[1] In its tools, techniques, and format, *The Saint John's Bible* revives the great medieval tradition of Christian illuminated Bibles largely lost since the Gutenberg Bible of the 1450s. Yet it also stands as a doorway into a dynamic tradition of Catholic biblical interpretation that predates the great medieval manuscripts and is perfectly suited to address the problem of how to read the Bible in our own era. In its use of iconography both ancient and modern, this Bible creates intertextual connections between different books of the canon. These connections cluster around contemporary issues, sparking the ethical and sacramental imaginations of this Bible's readers and viewers through *beautiful persuasion*.

MULTIPLE LEVELS OF MEANING, VISUAL EXEGESIS, AND ICONOGRAPHY

Michael Patella, OSB, the New Testament scholar who served as the head of the Committee, describes this Bible as a "premodern answer to a

---

1. The Committee on Illumination and Text (CIT) served as the liaison between Saint John's Abbey, the patron of *The Saint John's Bible*, and Donald Jackson, the Artistic Director of the project. The CIT gave theological and exegetical guidance to complement Jackson's artistic expertise.

1

postmodern question."[2] Since the Second Vatican Council, Catholic biblical scholarship has turned to historical criticism: the *human* authors of the Bible, their diversity, and their contexts. At root, historical criticism seeks to uncover the supposedly *original* meaning of biblical texts in their earliest historical setting. Such research has given us a much better understanding of the Bible's human authors and their contexts.

Historical criticism *alone*, however, has limits for a believing community that sees the Bible as more than just literature or historical documents. Historical criticism can dissect the Bible into parts while ignoring its unity, and it often neglects the divine author that gives the Bible that unity. For a historical critic, for example, Isaiah cannot be read through the lens of Paul, or Job through the lens of Genesis. Without denying the unique voices of the Bible's many human authors, solely focusing on the diversity of the Bible is inadequate for communities that accept the canon as normative for practice and nourishment for faith. The Bible may be diverse, but it must also speak as a whole.

The limits of historical criticism as an attempt at a unifying paradigm in Catholic biblical scholarship have led to Patella's "postmodern problem": To what interpretive tools and traditions should the church turn to gain its spiritual nourishment in Scripture? Patella joins a number of Catholic biblical scholars who have suggested a return to the "premodern answer": reveling in the *multiple possibilities and meanings* of Scripture just as patristic and medieval interpreters did.[3] In the medieval formulation of the *Quadriga*, Scripture contained four levels of meaning: the literal, the allegorical, the moral, and the anagogical.[4]

The stunningly contemporary art of *The Saint John's Bible* suggests many levels of meaning in Scripture. By juxtaposing ancient biblical text with modern art, *The Saint John's Bible* immediately suggests multiple layers and levels of meaning in Scripture. The art lies on the page not as a wooden illustration of the text but, in Patella's words, as a "spiritual meditation" on the text, a conversation partner for readers and viewers.[5] And the art of this Bible is itself diverse. The Orthodox icons of Aidan Hart, the meticulously illus-

---

2. Patella, *Word and Image*, 17.

3. Luke Timothy Johnson and William S. Kurz, *The Future of Catholic Biblical Scholarship: A Constructive Conversation* (Grand Rapids, MI: Eerdmans, 2002), 30–32, 57–59.

4. Pontifical Biblical Commission, *The Interpretation of the Bible in the Church* (Vatican City: Libreria Editrice Vaticana, 1993), III.B.1–3; Patella, *Word and Image*, 25.

5. Susan Sink, *The Art of* The Saint John's Bible: *The Complete Reader's Guide* (Collegeville, MN: Liturgical Press, 2013), xiv.

trated bugs of Chris Tomlin, and the abstract style of Suzanne Moore would seem not to make sense together in one Bible. Yet with Donald Jackson as the conductor of this symphony, they do. Suzanne Moore, one of the artists on the project, reflects that "the rhythm of the lettering, and paired with the artists' varying approaches and interpretations, came together in the seven volumes in a musical way: harmonizing, complementing, and sparking off of one another to create a unified and unexpected whole."[6] As art historian Travis Nygard describes it, "the multiplicity of imagery, artistic voices, and styles implies an endorsement of a plurality of approaches to the Bible."[7] If the Bible itself reflects different human authors and styles, why should an illuminated Bible not do so as well?

This theological insight coincides with biblical scholars' recent turn to *visual exegesis*: the way in which art interprets Scripture. The visual exegete reads the Bible and art based on the Bible side by side to raise questions about Scripture and explore new interpretive possibilities. As J. Cheryl Exum writes, art "can point to problematic aspects of the text and help us 'see' things about the text we might have overlooked, or enable us to see things differently."[8] For example, when David sends for Bathsheba to come to his palace, the biblical narrative does not tell us how she felt. But artists fill in that detail. Rembrandt, in *Bathing Bathsheba* (1654), gives us a fearful and uncomfortable victim. But in his *Bathsheba at the Fountain* (1635), Peter Paul Rubens portrays a Bathsheba excited at the chance to "trade up" her husband for the king.[9] Through the artists' eyes we turn back to the Bible with new insights.

When looking at any work of art, especially sacred art, *iconography* is an important tool. Iconography is a method in art history that identifies repeated motifs and symbols and analyzes their meanings within a work of

6. Christopher Calderhead, *Illuminating the Word: The Making of* The Saint John's Bible, 2nd ed. (Collegeville, MN: Liturgical Press, 2015), 281.

7. Travis Nygard, "Beautiful Persuasion in Christian Texts: An Analysis of Imagery in the *Moralized Ovid* and *Saint John's Bible* Manuscripts" (paper presented at Midwest Conference on Christianity and Literature, Spring Arbor University, Spring Arbor, MI, February 19–20, 2016).

8. J. Cheryl Exum, "Toward a Genuine Dialogue between the Bible and Art," in *Congress Volume Helsinki 2010*, ed. Martti Nissinen, Supplements to Vetus Testamentum 148 (Leiden: Brill, 2012), 474.

9. J. Cheryl Exum, *Plotted, Shot, and Painted: Cultural Representations of Biblical Women*, Journal for the Study of the Old Testament Supplement Series 215 (Sheffield, UK: Sheffield Academic Press, 1996), chap. 1, "Bathsheba Plotted, Shot, and Painted."

art or cultural tradition.[10] Christian art, like the art of many religions, has developed a highly nuanced and complex iconographic language. For example, the fish is one of the earliest symbols in Christian art. We can discern many associations with the fish:[11]

- One Greek word for fish, *ichthus*, is used as an acronym for "Jesus Christ, God, Son, Savior";
- A fish swallowed Jonah and he came out alive, often seen as a prefigurement of Jesus;
- Fish symbolize baptism: fish require water for life just as Christians require water to enter New Life;
- The gall of a fish restored the sight of Tobit in the deuterocanonical book of Tobit;
- In saints' iconography, fish serve as attributes of St. Simon the Zealot, St. Peter the fisherman, and St. Anthony of Padua, who preached to the fish;
- Fish can symbolize Satan, drawing from the sea monster Leviathan in Job and Isaiah.

This is not to say that *all* of those associations are included in *every* use of the fish in Christian art. But often, an artist plays with multiple associations of a symbol. An iconographer explores this complex symbolic language to understand better what artists are conveying in his or her work.

Identifying the symbols in a work of art, however, is not enough. One must then ask what a symbol means in the context of a specific artwork. How is the artist deploying it to make a broader point? *The Saint John's Bible* uses multiple symbols of fish in several illuminations. The most common is an image of a fish drawn from a Byzantine mosaic in the Benedictine monastery at Tabgha. This symbol appears in *Loaves and Fishes* (Mark 6:33-44; 8:1-10), *Creation* (Gen 1:1–2:3), *Elijah and the Fiery Chariot* (2 Kgs 2:1-14), *Son of Man* (Rev 1:12-20), and *Heavenly Choir* (Rev 4:8). This icon of a fish is significant because Tabgha, situated on the shore of the Sea of Galilee, is by tradition the location of the feeding story in Mark 6:33-44. In *Creation*, Donald Jackson includes two other fish images: one drawn from an ancient

10. Anne D'Alleva, *Methods & Theories of Art History*, 2nd ed. (London: Laurence King Publishing, 2012), 19–26.

11. George Ferguson, *Signs and Symbols in Christian Art* (London: Oxford University Press, 1961), 18; Alva William Steffler, *Symbols of the Christian Faith* (Grand Rapids, MI: Eerdmans, 2002), 9, 94.

fossil, and one a small depiction of a school of fish. These repeated symbols create connections between different illuminations and Scripture passages in *The Saint John's Bible*.

INTERTEXTUALITY AND THE UNITY AND HARMONY OF SCRIPTURE

Premodern exegesis, unlike historical criticism, affirms the unity of the Bible,[12] what Patella calls "the interrelatedness of individual biblical books with each other."[13] In Catholic teaching, the Bible is not just a collection of unrelated books, but "a gathering together of a whole array of witnesses from one great tradition."[14] Catholic exegetes must find the unifying threads and conversations that show the harmony of the canon of Scripture. This is especially obvious in the relationship of the New Testament to the Old: the New Testament would be incomprehensible without reference to the Old Testament.[15] The Committee advising *The Saint John's Bible* intended this project to reflect that unity of the Bible, "despite or rather because of its ambiguities, contradictions, and various errors in facts and details."[16]

Michael Patella suggests that a recent method for reading Scripture, *intertextuality*, echoes the insights of the early Church Fathers. Against the idea that any text can be read in a vacuum, intertextuality seeks to uncover

---

12. Johnson and Kurz, *The Future of Catholic Biblical Scholarship*, 47–55.

13. Patella, *Word and Image*, 14.

14. Pontifical Biblical Commission, *Interpretation of the Bible* I.C.

15. In this book, I use the terms *Old Testament* and *New Testament* to refer to the two major divisions of the Christian Scriptures. This reflects the fact that this book treats the Christian Bible as a unified work and often connects the Old Testament with the New. In Judaism, the correct term for their sacred scripture is "Tanakh," an acronym for Torah (Pentateuch), Nevi'im (Prophets), and Ketuvim (Writings). The Tanakh contains the same books as the Protestant Old Testament but in a different order. The Catholic Old Testament adds books to the Tanakh, including books written in Greek, making the popular term *Hebrew Bible* inappropriate for this study. When I use the term *Old Testament*, I do not mean to imply that it is outdated or irrelevant. In the words of Jewish New Testament scholar Amy-Jill Levine, I use the label to convey "something basic, something prime, and something essential." Amy-Jill Levine, "The Jewish People and Their Sacred Scriptures in the Bible" (lecture, Creighton University, November 2, 2014), https://www.youtube.com/watch?v=C_I8gw9ww5w.

16. Patella, *Word and Image*, 74.

every text's "inseparability from associations with other texts."[17] Every text exists in a thick web of other texts and cannot be fully understood apart from those allusions and references. Imagine trying to interpret a political cartoon from a hundred years ago. It would be quite difficult, since that satire makes sense only if one knows the context of the time. The intertexts—campaign speeches and slogans, candidates' mocked mannerisms, global and national events, and so forth—are necessary to comprehend fully the cartoon's joke.

Authors of texts create intertexts when they intentionally allude to other works. But *readers* also create intertexts through their associations, memories, and previous encounters with a text.[18] For example, when Paul cites Isaiah, that intertextual connection is created by the author. But many readers cannot help but call to mind Cecil B. DeMille's *The Ten Commandments* every time they encounter the book of Exodus. Reader-supplied intertexts are not only individual but communal. In the Catholic community, reader-generated intertexts are especially obvious in the way the Lectionary connects Old Testament, Psalms, Epistles, and Gospels every Sunday. Intertextuality also features in the Benedictine tradition of praying Scripture through *lectio divina*, a method used extensively by the Committee advising *The Saint John's Bible*.[19] This book focuses on such playful intertexts created by readers: both the Committee and the artists whose creative readings resulted in this Bible, and the readers of *The Saint John's Bible*.

The Saint John's Bible creates intertextuality through the use of repeated iconography. The intertextuality of *The Saint John's Bible* came from both the Committee on Illumination and Text's creative free associations and Donald Jackson's and the other artists' lexicon of visual leitmotifs that appear throughout the text.[20] Some of these symbols are drawn from ancient and medieval Christian art, such as the fish. Others, such as tanks, Buddhist mandalas, and DNA strands, are definitely from *our* time! The creators of this Bible intended to fashion a new visual lexicon of symbols for the project.[21] I am not arguing, however, that every connection discussed in this study was

17. Patricia K. Tull, "Rhetorical Criticism and Intertextuality," in *To Each Its Own Meaning: An Introduction to Biblical Criticisms and Their Application*, ed. Steven L. McKenzie and Stephen R. Haynes, rev. ed. (Louisville, KY: Westminster John Knox, 1999), 165.

18. G. D. Miller, "Intertextuality in Old Testament Research," *Currents in Biblical Research* 9, no. 3 (2011): 285–88.

19. Tim Gray, *Praying Scripture for a Change: An Introduction to Lectio Divina* (West Chester, PA: Ascension Press, 2009), 66–68.

20. Patella, *Word and Image*, chap. 4, "Leitmotifs"; Calderhead, *Illuminating the Word*, 112–13.

21. Calderhead, *Illuminating the Word*, 329–30; Patella, *Word and Image*, 15–17.

intended by its creators. Sometimes the Holy Spirit made things happen in this project that were not planned.[22]

The intertextual, iconographic connections in *The Saint John's Bible* are crucial in creating the rich conversations between several different illuminations. These "canonical conversations" create a dialogue between different parts of the Bible and all those who read this Bible: the Jews and Christians who center their lives around the Good Book and all of humanity made in God's image. Though we will look at only three, there are many canonical conversations possible using *The Saint John's Bible*.

SCRIPTURE, TRADITION, AND THE ETHICAL IMAGINATION

Catholic biblical exegesis, both ancient and modern, is rooted in the believing community and its tradition of interpretation.[23] The interpretation of Scripture is not a private affair solely between the believer and God; rather, "interpretation of Scripture takes place in the heart of the church . . . within its tradition of faith."[24] Observers of Catholic culture have noted its focus on the communal dimension of human life. Catholic biblical interpretation follows suit.

Reading Scripture in tradition is not merely repeating past interpretations or recycling previous commentaries. Tradition cannot remain static, because life is not static. Christians, like all people of faith, continually face new challenges. As *Dei Verbum* notes, "The tradition that comes from the apostles makes progress in the church, with the help of the holy Spirit. There is a growth in insight into the realities and words that are being passed on" (8).[25] For example, the Bible says nothing directly about cloning, yet Christians turn to the Bible and other parts of the Christian tradition to discern how to react to such complex bioethical issues. The council fathers go on to explain that this "growth in insight" comes from contemplation and study. This contemplation and study, under the guidance of the Holy Spirit, enables us to discern how to understand and live out Scripture in the light of our times.

---

22. Michael Patella, personal communication, August 6, 2016.

23. Daniel J. Harrington, *How Do Catholics Read the Bible?* (Lanham, MD: Rowman & Littlefield, 2005), 106–11.

24. Pontifical Biblical Commission, *Interpretation of the Bible* III.A.3.

25. Dogmatic Constitution on Divine Revelation (*Dei Verbum*), November 18, 1965, in *Vatican Council II: Constitutions, Decrees, Declarations; The Basic Sixteen Documents*, ed. Austin Flannery (Collegeville, MN: Liturgical Press, 2014), 102.

The process of creating *The Saint John's Bible* was inherently ecclesial. *The Saint John's Bible* is a vision not only of Donald Jackson and his team of artists but also of the Committee on Illumination and Text (CIT), a committee of biblical scholars, theologians, artists, and art historians mostly based at Saint John's University. Drawing on their scholarly expertise and their *lectio divina* sessions, the CIT drafted briefs suggesting theological themes on which each illumination might focus, while giving Jackson and the other artists much leeway for creativity. Each illumination is a product of a rich conversation between the artists and the Committee representing the Catholic, Benedictine tradition.

The Saint John's Bible announces its retrieval of the medieval tradition of *giant* illuminated Bibles before one even opens its two-feet-tall pages. In those pages, one finds frequent ecclesial symbolism, particularly symbols related to the monks of Saint John's Abbey who were the patrons of this Bible.[26] Through the Daily Office, these monks pray the entire Psalter communally every four weeks. Donald Jackson's *Psalms Frontispiece* reflects these prayers' prominence in the monks' spiritual life.

The illumination underscores the communal, chanted, liturgical dimension of the Psalms in monastic life, as opposed to a private, silent reading. Oscillographs—visual representations of sound waves—of the monks of Saint John's Abbey chanting the Psalms line every page. The frontispiece contains the motif of the double doors of the Cathedral of Saint James at Compostela, reminding the viewer of the many churches where the Psalms are chanted. The cross in the center, made up of five squares, alludes to the large bell tower of Saint John's Abbey Church. Other architectural motifs from Saint John's University appear throughout *The Saint John's Bible*. The small Stella Maris Chapel shows up in *Life in Community* and *Paul Anthology*, both in Acts. The bold Bauhaus architecture of Saint John's Abbey Church appears in *Pentecost* and *Faithful Friends* (Sir 6:14-22). The Sacred Heart Chapel from the College of Saint Benedict, Saint John's University's sister school, stands in the background of *Pillars of Wisdom* (Prov 8:22–9:6). Minnesotan flora and fauna decorate the pages of the manuscript.[27] These symbols of the monks' liturgical prayer and its location remind the viewer that this Bible was created by a *particular* community and reflects the faith of that community—even as it is a gift for all Christians and for the entire world.

---

26. Patella, *Word and Image*, 76.
27. Sink, *The Art of* The Saint John's Bible, 12.

Donald Jackson, *Psalms Frontispiece*

As the church confronts new issues in the world, it brings Scripture and the other sources of its tradition to bear on those issues by employing the *ethical imagination*. This is the capacity to see how the Gospel can apply to the circumstances of the world around us. It is a necessary component of what the Pontifical Biblical Commission refers to as "actualization," the process of rereading Scripture "in the light of new circumstances and appl[ying it] to the contemporary situation of the people of God."[28] This process entails

28. Pontifical Biblical Commission, *Interpretation of the Bible* IV.A.

three steps: "hear[ing] the word from within one's own concrete situation," "identify[ing] the aspects of the present situation highlighted or put in question by the biblical text," and "draw[ing] from the fullness of meaning contained in the biblical text those elements capable of advancing the present situation in a way that is productive and consonant with the saving will of God in Christ." Hearing, identifying, and drawing on Scripture lifts it out of the shadowy past and throws it into the center of the ills and tragedies of our own time.

While the "concrete situation" of the interpreter of Scripture could be her own life, it could also be social-political issues such as protection of the vulnerable, women's rights, world peace, and creation care.[29] For example, Pope Francis in *Laudato Si'* actualizes Scripture to speak to the ethical problem of environmental destruction. His encyclical begins with a close look at the scientific research on and geopolitical context of this ecological crisis—the concrete situation to which he then applies Scripture and other parts of the Catholic tradition. Actualization is not merely a matter of just reading the Bible. It requires bridging the gap between the Bible's time and our own. And this bridging begins with imagination to discern a problem and make Scripture speak to it with creative fidelity.

For Michael Patella, the ethical dimension of the Bible—the medieval "moral sense" of Scripture—leads to a next step: "Our experience with Sacred Scripture should prod us to transform this world into the kingdom of God."[30] The moral sense of Scripture brings us directly to our union with Christ—the anagogical sense. When we live out the ethical imagination applied to the Bible, we become like Christ, who interpreted the Tanakh—the Jewish Bible—for his own time and place. *The Saint John's Bible* is a visual record of the church's tradition of biblical interpretation at the dawn of the third millennium. The *art* of *The Saint John's Bible* becomes a resource for the ethical imagination today.

THE SACRAMENTAL IMAGINATION AND BEAUTIFUL PERSUASION

The Saint John's Bible sparks the ethical imaginations of its viewers and readers through what art historian Travis Nygard calls "beautiful persuasion."[31] This Bible inspires the ethical imagination *through* its beauty,

---

29. Ibid., IV.A.2.
30. Patella, *Word and Image*, 25.
31. Nygard, "Beautiful Persuasion in Christian Texts."

which draws our attention. In Catholic culture, beauty also acts as a conduit for God's love through the *sacramental imagination*, which holds that God is immanent, intimately present in all creation, rather than transcendent and distant. As Andrew Greeley suggests,

> The objects, events, and persons of ordinary existence hint at the nature of God and indeed make God in some fashion present to us. . . . Everything in creation, from the exploding cosmos to the whirling, dancing, and utterly mysterious quantum particles, discloses something about God and, in so doing, brings God among us.[32]

Greeley shows how the sacramental imagination is embodied in the rich heritage of Catholic art, architecture, opera, music, and other forms of creative expression—including, of course, liturgy. The sacramental imagination treasures images, analogies, metaphors, and sacred spaces and times as wide varieties of ways to express facets of the mystery of God's nature. Sacramentality is more than just the seven liturgical sacraments, but, in the words of Michael Himes, "any person, place, thing, or event, any sight, sound, taste, touch, or smell that causes us to notice the love which supports all that exists, that undergirds your being and mine and the being of everything about us. How many such sacraments are there? The number is virtually infinite."[33] Art can be a sacrament; so can friendship and flowers. The root reality of the Catholic sacramental imagination is that God is *love*. No image of God, no metaphor for God can contradict this boundary.

The multiplication of metaphors, images, and other finite pointers to God never quite gets us all the way to God, who is always beyond our imagining.[34] Thus, cultivating the sacramental imagination involves finding new meaning in old metaphors and images for God, and creating new ones entirely—always remembering the most basic, fundamental truth that God is love.[35] As Himes puts it, "the whole Catholic sacramental life is a training to be beholders" of God's grace, a "lifelong pedagogy to bring us to see what

32. Andrew Greeley, *The Catholic Imagination* (Berkeley: University of California Press, 2001), 6–7.

33. Michael Himes, "Finding God in All Things: A Sacramental Worldview and Its Effects," in *Becoming Beholders: Cultivating Sacramental Imagination and Actions in College Classrooms*, ed. Karen E. Eifler and Thomas M. Landy (Collegeville, MN: Michael Glazier, 2014), 13.

34. Ibid., 5.

35. Ibid., 9.

is there."[36] Faith is not merely about believing in creeds and theological orthodoxies; it is cultivating the imagination to see grace present everywhere, or, as St. Ignatius puts it, to find God in all things.

The Saint John's Bible cultivates the sacramental imagination through both its beautiful imagery and its skillful calligraphy, which help the viewer-reader to see the grace of God expressed in the words of Scripture. John Klassen, OSB, the abbot of Saint John's Abbey when the project was begun, remarks that *The Saint John's Bible* is "a retrieval of the Catholic imagination with Scripture. The Word becomes sacramental. It is not just a text. It is like the Eucharist: a visual image of the Word."[37] The skill and precision of the calligraphy draws attention to the Word as it points to God. This Bible is not just disembodied words, but the Word "enfleshed" in vellum, ink, paint, and gold leaf. The sheer size of *The Saint John's Bible*—two feet by three feet when opened—reminds us how large the Bible figuratively looms in Christianity, and how difficult it can be to carry the Bible into a new generation and actualize it for new times.

The Saint John's Bible combines the ethical and sacramental imaginations to invite the viewer-reader into the biblical world and bring Scripture to bear on questions of justice. The key word here is "invite." Propaganda, whether TV advertisements or political slogans, demands that its audience do a concrete action: buy a product, vote for a candidate. Propaganda is mere manipulation of emotions, not empowerment for one's own conscience and action.[38] This is the opposite of Travis Nygard's "beautiful persuasion." Luke Timothy Johnson argues that biblical exegesis in the church should aim to cultivate the "scriptural imagination," to bring believers into the imaginative world of Scripture.[39] Given that "people are drawn to beauty, and beauty is a reflection of the glory of God,"[40] what better way to invite people into the world of Scripture than through beautiful art? As Catholic Scripture scholar Stephen Binz writes, "We don't just study scripture; we assimilate it. We take it in, eat it, chew it, digest it."[41] And what better way to digest

36. Ibid., 14.

37. Calderhead, *Illuminating the Word*, 23.

38. Christopher McMahon, "Image and Narrative: Reflections on the Theological Significance of *The Saint John's Bible*," *American Benedictine Review* 58, no. 1 (2007): 37–38.

39. Johnson and Kurz, *The Future of Catholic Biblical Scholarship*, 131–42.

40. Michael Patella, "Looking into the Bible," in *Becoming Beholders: Cultivating Sacramental Imagination and Actions in College Classrooms*, ed. Karen E. Eifler and Thomas M. Landy (Collegeville, MN: Michael Glazier, 2014), 141.

41. Stephen J. Binz, *Transformed by God's Word: Discovering the Power of Lectio and Visio Divina* (Notre Dame, IN: Ave Maria Press, 2016), 5.

spiritual food than a multisensory Bible that can be heard with the ears, touched with the fingers, viewed with the eyes, and read with the intellect? *The Saint John's Bible* invites through *beauty*—a beauty that becomes even more apparent once the viewer teases out its intertextual, iconographic canonical conversations. With this framework in place, we now enter three of these conversations.

Chapter Two

JESUS' FAMILY TREE
Peace between Jews and Christians

Religious art, past and present, speaks volumes concerning Jewish-Christian relations. In medieval Christian art, sculptures contrasting church and synagogue featured two women, *Ecclesia* and *Synagoga*, representing the two religious traditions. While *Ecclesia* stood triumphantly in the truth, *Synagoga* was often blindfolded and bowing to her counterpart.[1] As Catholic theology about Judaism changed, so has Catholic art about *Synagoga*. In his survey of the past fifty years of Jewish-Catholic dialogue, *Seeking Shalom*, Catholic theologian Philip Cunningham includes on the cover an image of Joshua Koffman's sculpture *Synagoga and Ecclesia in Our Time*.[2]

In Koffman's work, commissioned by Saint Joseph's University in Philadelphia to mark the golden jubilee of *Nostra Aetate*, the two women sit side by side. *Synagoga* reads her companion's Bible while *Ecclesia* reads her companion's Torah scroll. While medieval depictions of *Synagoga* portray her with a broken crown, Koffman's personifications both wear crowns. When Pope Francis blessed the sculpture during his 2015 visit to the U.S., his friend Rabbi Abraham Skorka turned to him and proclaimed, "They are you and I, pope and rabbi learning from each other."[3] Triumphalism has changed to mutual worship of God.[4]

---

1. Mary C. Boys, *Has God Only One Blessing? Judaism as a Source of Christian Self-Understanding* (New York: Paulist Press, 2000), chap. 3, "Synagoga and Ecclesia."

2. Philip A. Cunningham, *Seeking Shalom: The Journey to Right Relationship between Catholics and Jews* (Grand Rapids, MI: Eerdmans, 2015).

3. Joshua Koffman, personal communication, July 13, 2017.

4. Judith Bookbinder, "Synagoga and Ecclesia in Our Time: A Transformative Sculptural Statement in Traditional Form," *Studies in Christian-Jewish Relations* 11, no. 1 (2016).

Joshua Koffman, *Synagoga and Ecclesia in Our Time* (2015)

The decades since the Holocaust have seen the Catholic Church's conversion to this new way of engaging with Jews and Judaism. This consisted in a shift away from old polemics against the Jews as a people condemned as Christ-killers, their Torah considered superseded or replaced by Christian grace, to a new openness to God's ongoing covenant with the Jews and the church's need to emphasize God's love for the Jews. This new relationship with Judaism was marked substantively by ecclesial documents beginning with Vatican II's *Nostra Aetate*, new engagements with Jews in biblical scholarship, and ecclesial neighborliness, including the famous relationship between John Paul II and Elio Toaff, the chief rabbi of Rome.

The Saint John's Bible reflects and amplifies this new openness to Jews and Judaism. It signals how that openness to Judaism has played out in Catholic biblical scholarship and a more sensitive approach to issues of supersessionism, typology, God's continuing covenant with the Jews, and the Jewishness of Jesus and Paul. This Bible's openness to Jews and Judaism is not only a product of its use of Jewish symbols but is also revealed in the stories surrounding the creation of this unique Bible. To begin our journey through *The Saint John's Bible* and Judaism, let us consider the first illumination of this Bible shown to the public: the full-page illumination of Jesus' family tree beginning the Gospel of Matthew.

MATTHEW'S MENORAH

> Matthew 1:1-17: *Genealogy of Jesus*
> Matthew 1: Decorative cross
> Romans 5: Decorative cross

At the start of *The Saint John's Bible*'s production, Donald Jackson was first commissioned with producing a full-page illumination of Matthew's genealogy. This would be the first illumination delivered to the monks at Saint John's Abbey, and the first seen by the public. As Jackson later recollected this opening work, he described his mood as "dread."[5] This illumination, which would set the tone for the rest of the project, contains a powerful affirmation of Judaism.

Jackson intended to foreground Christianity's relationship with Judaism through the menorah, a symbol of Judaism since ancient times, as the shape of Jesus' family tree. As Jackson described it, "My idea was to suggest a bridge between the Old Testament and the New, so I used the menorah as a foundation of the design to acknowledge Christianity's Jewish roots."[6] This illumination emphasizes Christianity's debt to Judaism and Jesus' own Jewishness. In doing so, *The Saint John's Bible* follows the lead of the church. The United States Conference of Catholic Bishops' 1988 document on producing passion plays without anti-Jewish polemic specifies that "the menorah, tablets of the law, and other Jewish symbols should appear throughout the play and be connected with Jesus."[7]

The illumination also hints at dialogue with religions beyond Judaism. The menorah contains mandala patterns from Tibetan Buddhism and arabesque designs from Islamic manuscript art. Jackson wanted not only to highlight Judaism but also to draw out "a kinship with other spiritual teachers," suggesting the "connectedness of all seekers of enlightenment. All paths lead to God."[8] The arabesque designs at the top, which serve as the flames of the menorah, signal the tree reaching up to the light—the gold leaf that represents divinity.[9] Still, the dominance of the menorah signals a focus on Judaism.

5. Calderhead, *Illuminating the Word*, 163.

6. Ibid., 165.

7. Bishops' Committee for Ecumenical and Interreligious Affairs, United States Conference of Catholic Bishops, *Criteria for the Evaluation of Dramatizations of the Passion* (1988), B.3.i.

8. Quoted in Calderhead, *Illuminating the Word*, 165.

9. Ferguson, *Signs and Symbols in Christian Art*, 42.

Donald Jackson, Matthew 1:1-17: *Genealogy of Jesus*

The Saint John's Bible's connection between the menorah and Jesus underscores Jesus' Jewish roots. The genealogy in Matthew 1 "situate[s] Jesus in relation to the memorable characters in Israel's history," establishing Jesus' lineage as a descendant of Abraham and David.[10] The DNA strands between the arms of the menorah point to the significance of heredity in passing on Jewish identity, and remind us that Jesus was a flesh-and-blood human with human DNA, that God works through "the 'mundane' or normalcy of the human realities reflected in a genealogy."[11] One might also note the absence of a DNA strand next to Joseph.[12] Jackson also adds the names of the women of Jesus' family tree, while Matthew omits most of them. Their DNA was key for Jesus as well.

The DNA strands also allude to familial metaphors for the relationship between Jews and Christians in recent Catholic teaching. In a 1986 address to the synagogue of Rome, John Paul II remarked, "You are our dearly beloved brothers, and in a certain way, it could be said that you are our elder brothers."[13] In 2015, another Vatican document referred to Jews and Christians as "two siblings who—as is the normal course of events for siblings—have developed in different directions."[14] Benedict XVI used a different familial metaphor, referring to the Jews as Christians' "fathers in faith."[15] These familial images take shape in the DNA strands, a fact not lost on Jewish observers of this Bible. One ambassador for the project, calligrapher Anne Kaese, recounts her experience showing this illumination at a synagogue:

> One lady saw [*Genealogy of Jesus*] as a statement of outreach and upliftment of the Jewish heritage. She felt vindicated at some level that Judaism was the cornerstone or foundation of the Christian and Muslim faiths in some ways. She liked that the DNA crawled over the menorah and saw that as making her faith alive and present in all peoples.[16]

---

10. Barbara E. Reid, "The Gospel According to Matthew," in *New Collegeville Bible Commentary: New Testament*, ed. Daniel Durken (Collegeville, MN: Liturgical Press, 2009), 8.

11. Lawrence Fraher, personal communication, July 19, 2017.

12. I am indebted to David Pleins for this observation.

13. John Paul II, "Address at the Great Synagogue of Rome" (homily, Great Synagogue of Rome, April 13, 1986), http://www.nytimes.com/1986/04/14/world/text-of-pope-s -speech-at-rome-synagogue-you-are-our-elder-brothers.html.

14. Commission of the Holy See for Religious Relations with the Jews, *"The Gifts and the Calling of God Are Irrevocable" (Rom 11:29): A Reflection on Theological Questions Pertaining to Catholic-Jewish Relations* (December 10, 2015), 2.15.

15. Ibid.

16. Anne Kaese, personal communication, May 25, 2017.

In its attention to the Jewish viewer-reader of the project, *The Saint John's Bible* facilitates Jewish-Christian understanding.

But this bond between Jews and Christians was more than just artistic flourish. Jewish dialogue partners gave their input on this illumination. The Committee was understandably hesitant to use Jewish imagery without Jewish input! Committee member and art historian Johanna Becker recounted that "a member of the committee talked to a rabbi, discussing the mixture of images—the menorah, the tree of life, the genealogy of Christ. He gave the okay."[17] When Jackson was transporting the illumination to be unveiled to the public for the first time at the Minneapolis Institute of Art, he panicked, worrying that some Jews might feel the image was appropriation. He related:

> We showed the page to Evan Mauer who was at that time the director of the [Minneapolis Institute of Art] and was a great supporter of the project from the start. He is also a devout Jew. He turned to Brother Dietrich [the president of Saint John's University] and said, "We are all men of the book. We must have The Saint John's Bible on exhibit here."[18]

In both the creation of this Bible and its initial unveiling, Jewish voices lent their support of and appreciation for the project.

On the opposite page from the menorah stands a cross, another allusion to the continuity between Judaism and Christianity. This cross harkens forward to a similar cross in Romans. Paul's letter to the Romans serves as a key source for the new Christian theology of Judaism, as it contains one of the most potent pro-Jewish texts in the New Testament.

While John Paul II describes the relationship between Judaism and Christianity in terms of siblinghood, Paul uses the image of an olive tree in Romans 11 to connect Judaism and Christianity:

> Paul coined the expressive image of the root of Israel into which the wild branches of the Gentiles have been grafted (cf. Rom 11:16-21). . . . This image represents for Paul the decisive key to thinking of the relationship between Israel and the Church in the light of faith.[19]

Paul describes Judaism and Christianity as two branches of the same olive tree, an image we can extend to the menorah in *Genealogy of Jesus*. Biblically,

17. Calderhead, *Illuminating the Word*, 118.
18. Ibid., 165.
19. Commission for Religious Relations with the Jews, *"The Gifts and the Calling of God Are Irrevocable" (Rom 11:29)*, 5.35.

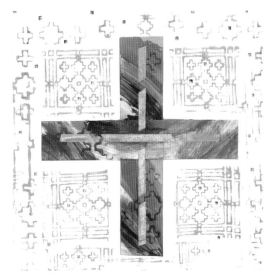

Donald Jackson, Matthew 1: Decorative cross   Donald Jackson, Romans 5: Decorative cross

the menorah, the seven-branched lamp in the temple, is symbolically related to plants. The book of Exodus describes the construction of the menorah as having "branches" and cups shaped like almond blossoms (25:31-40). *The Jewish Study Bible* suggests that "it resembled a stylized tree, possibly symbolizing fertility or the sustenance of life."[20] The menorah's association with the tree may also stem from the sacred tree imagery common in the ancient Near East, the cosmic tree at the center of the earth rooted in the underworld and reaching up to the realm of the gods.[21] Perhaps the menorah-tree in the temple evokes and replaces sacred trees associated with worship of the goddess Asherah.[22] In *Genealogy of Jesus*, the menorah-tree, rooted in the name of Hagar, reaches up to the golden geometric patterns drawn from Islamic art. The tree hints at Islam's presence with Judaism and Christianity in the Abrahamic family tree.

20. Adele Berlin and Marc Zvi Brettler, eds., *The Jewish Study Bible*, 2nd ed. (Oxford: Oxford University Press, 2014).

21. Leon Yarden, *The Tree of Light: A Study of the Menorah, The Seven-Branched Lampstand* (Ithaca, NY: Cornell University Press, 1971), chap. 5, "The Sacred Tree."

22. Mark S. Smith, "The Book of Exodus," in *New Collegeville Bible Commentary: Old Testament*, ed. Daniel Durken (Collegeville, MN: Liturgical Press, 2015), Kindle Locations 3791–3795.

The mandala designs in Matthew's menorah resurface in *Garden of Eden*, linking the menorah as a family tree of fertility and the Tree of Life in the Garden.[23] Medieval Christian art traditionally used an image of the tree of Jesse to symbolize Jesus' genealogy, drawing from Isaiah's messianic prediction that "a shoot shall come out from the stock of Jesse, and a branch shall grow out of his roots" (Isa 11:1).[24] *The Saint John's Bible* connects the menorah as family tree—the tree of Jesse—with Paul's olive tree and Adam and Eve's Tree of Life. The tree also supplies the wood for the cross.

MENORAHS AND THE SURVIVAL OF THE CHOSEN PEOPLE, FROM ABRAHAM TO THE SHOAH

> Genesis 49: Decorative menorah
> Deuteronomy 34: Decorative menorah
> Ruth 4:17-22: *Ruth Genealogy*
> Proverbs 31:10-31: *Woman of Valor*
> Exodus 20:1-17: *The Ten Commandments*
> Joshua 4: *Choose This Day*
> Ezekiel 37:1-14: *Valley of the Dry Bones*
> Genesis 15 and 17: *The Call of Abraham*
> Psalms: *Psalms Frontispiece*

The illuminations in *The Saint John's Bible* are rich in meaning, but their full meaning reveals itself through the symbols repeated in many illuminations. The menorah in *Genealogy of Jesus* harks back to several other menorahs in Old Testament illuminations, all of which multiply the menorah's meaning as a symbol of the survival of the Jewish people through painful situations.

Even apart from *The Saint John's Bible*, the menorah symbolizes the continuation of the Jewish people.[25] In the contemporary North American context, it is best known for its ritual use during Hanukkah, which commemorates the Maccabean Revolt in Hellenistic Jewish times. Hanukkah celebrates the menorah in the temple miraculously burning for seven days

---

23. Lawrence Fraher, "The Illuminated Imagination: Layered Metaphor in *The Saint John's Bible* Frontispiece *Genealogy of Christ*" (unpublished manuscript, May 2, 2014), 6.

24. Ferguson, *Signs and Symbols in Christian Art*, 39.

25. Ellen Frankel and Betsy Platkin Teutsch, *The Encyclopedia of Jewish Symbols* (Northvale, NJ: Jason Aronson, 1995), 105–7.

despite having only a small amount of oil. This holiday is thus a reminder of God's work in keeping the Jewish people alive. Apart from its description in biblical accounts of Solomon's temple, archaeologists have shown that the menorah is associated with Jewish sites since at least the first century CE.[26] Not only does the menorah symbolize the survival of the Jewish people, the menorah as a symbol itself has also survived for two millennia!

In *The Saint John's Bible*, the menorah likewise signifies the survival of the Jewish people. It first appears on the cover of the Heritage Edition of the Pentateuch volume[27] and later appears at the ends of Genesis, Deuteronomy, and Ruth, symbolizing the family tree of the patriarchs, the survival of the Israelites in the desert, and the place of Ruth in Jesus' genealogy.

These three menorahs, all shaped in a tapestry-like pattern, evoke *Woman of Valor* (Prov 31:10-31). This illumination, created by Hazel Dolby, is shaped like a hanging tapestry. In *The Saint John's Bible*, textiles symbolize the presence of women, who are required for any family tree.[28] Just as *Genealogy of Jesus* adds the names of the women in Jesus' ancestry—names omitted in Matthew's text—this Bible again connects the survival of the Jewish people with the *women* who make that survival possible.

In the book of Exodus, God works powerful miracles to bring the Jewish people out of slavery. Thomas Ingmire's *Ten Commandments* text treatment alludes to one of these miracles: Moses' burning bush.

26. Steven Fine, *The Menorah: From the Bible to Modern Israel* (Cambridge, MA: Harvard University Press, 2016), chap. 1.

27. Every volume of the Heritage Edition of *The Saint John's Bible* has a different motif on the cover. These motifs symbolize one main theme of that volume.

28. Patella, *Word and Image*, 81.

sons, has borne him." [16] Then Naomi took the child and laid him in her bosom, and became his nurse. [17] The women of the neighborhood gave him a name, saying, "A son has been born to Naomi." They named him Obed; he became the father of Jesse, the father of David. [18] Now these are the descendants of Perez: Perez became the father of Hezron, [19] Hezron of Ram, Ram of Amminadab, [20] Amminadab of Nahshon, Nahshon of Salmon, [21] Salmon of Boaz, Boaz of Obed, [22] Obed of Jesse, and Jesse of David.

[17] THE WOMEN OF THE NEIGHBORHOOD GAVE HIM A NAME, SAYING, "A SON HAS BEEN BORN TO NAOMI." THEY NAMED HIM OBED; HE BECAME THE FATHER OF JESSE, THE FATHER OF DAVID. [18] NOW THESE ARE THE DESCENDANTS OF PEREZ; PEREZ BECAME THE FATHER OF HEZRON. HEZRON OF RAM. RAM OF AMMINADAB. AMMINADAB OF NAHSHON. NAHSHON OF SALMON. [21] SALMON OF BOAZ. BOAZ OF OBED. OBED OF JESSE, AND JESSE OF DAVID.

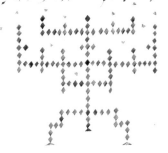

Donald Jackson,
Ruth 4:17-22: *Ruth Genealogy*

Thomas Ingmire, Exodus 20:1-17: *The Ten Commandments*

Thomas Ingmire, Exodus 20:1-17: *The Ten Commandments*, sketch

Early sketches in preparation for this work reveal that the burning bush was first conceived as a conventional menorah.[29] In the final version of this illumination, Ingmire abstracted the menorah to look like the burning bush.[30] The burning bush becomes the menorah, evoking the connection between menorahs and trees, between the bush that burned without being consumed and the Hanukkah lamp.

The menorah appears again in the Historical Books to represent key times when the Jews' survival was questionable. Though the image is located at Joshua 4, the text it reflects is Joshua 24:15, Joshua's speech at Shechem to the Israelites. Joshua forces the question: Will you choose the Egyptian gods or the God of Israel?

29. Calderhead, *Illuminating the Word*, 201.
30. Thomas Ingmire, personal communication, June 1, 2017.

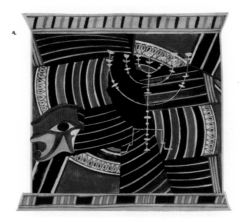

Donald Jackson, Joshua 4: *Choose This Day*

The illumination contrasts the eye of Horus with the menorah to represent this choice.[31] Finally, Donald Jackson's *Esther* contrasts her dual identities as royal Persian queen and secret Jew. The illumination visualizes this contrast using Persian iconography, traditional Palestinian women's ornament, and the symbol of the menorah. This symbol of survival embodies Esther's bravery in averting a genocide against the Jews of Persia.

Jackson's illumination of Ezekiel's vision of the valley of the dry bones connects the menorah with the largest threat in recent history to the survival of the Jews: the Shoah, also known as the Holocaust. This horrific historical fact looms in the background of the church's coming to terms with its relationship with the Jews, which began in a major way partly because of Christians' complicity in the genocide of the Jews of Europe. The Israelite prophet Ezekiel uses the image of dead bones being enfleshed and resurrected to symbolize the restoration of Israel: "Just as God has created life, so too can the Lord revivify Israel."[32] In *Valley of the Dry Bones*, Jackson represents the bones using images of twentieth-century genocides in Armenia, Rwanda, Iraq, Bosnia, Cambodia, and Europe. This last genocide, the Shoah, is represented by a pile of eyeglasses.[33] The 1998 Vatican document

31. Calderhead, *Illuminating the Word*, 246.

32. Corrine L. Carvalho, "The Book of Ezekiel," in *New Collegeville Bible Commentary: Old Testament*, ed. Daniel Durken (Collegeville, MN: Liturgical Press, 2015), Kindle Location 28250.

33. For some of the images used as sources for this illumination, see Calderhead, *Illuminating the Word*, 220–21.

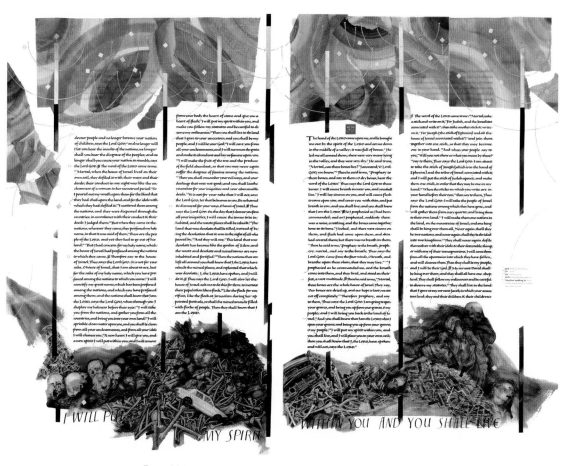

Donald Jackson, Ezekiel 37:1-14: *Valley of the Dry Bones*

We Remember: A Reflection on the Shoah draws the connection between centuries of Christian anti-Judaism and the racial ideology of Nazi anti-Semitism: "For Christians, this heavy burden of conscience of their brothers and sisters during the Second World War must be a call to penitence."[34] Rather than ignore or deny the past, the church repents of the complicity of many Christians in the Holocaust. In this illumination, the despair of the Shoah and other genocides is offset by the menorahs in the sky, a reminder that the Jewish people will continue.

34. Commission of the Holy See for Religious Relations with the Jews, *We Remember: A Reflection on the Shoah* (March 16, 1998), IV.

Donald Jackson, Genesis 15 and 17: *The Call of Abraham*

In *The Call of Abraham*, illuminating God's covenant with Abraham, Jackson again uses the menorah to represent the Abrahamic family tree. He paints large menorahs in the night sky alongside the golden names of the twelve tribes of Israel. He adds leaves to the "trunk" of the menorahs. God gives Abraham a family tree, a Tree of Life, through his promise to make Abraham's descendants grow as numerous as the stars in the sky (Gen 15:5). To add another layer: Zechariah's fifth vision of the lamp and the olive trees (Zech 4:1-14) describes the seven lamps of the menorah as "the eyes of the Lord, which range through the whole earth" (Zech 4:10), interpreted by

later Jewish exegetes as referring to the stars in the sky.[35] In the margins of this two-page spread, Jackson inserts a key phrase: "Look toward heaven and count the stars—so shall your descendants be" (Gen 15:5). Small Stars of David, a well-known symbol of Judaism, separate the two halves of this verse. The menorahs Abraham sees in the night sky are holding the candles that are the stars in the sky, and the stars in the sky are the Stars of David, and the Stars of David descend from Abraham in his family Tree of Life. The night sky and stars in this illumination appear again in Luke's *Crucifixion*.

35. Fine, *The Menorah*, 38–40.

In one case, the menorah symbolizes Jewish liturgy. The seven candle-lights atop the *Psalms Frontispiece* allude to the seven branches of the menorah. The Psalms frontispiece contains references to many religions in its use of oscillographs of Islamic, Buddhist, Hindu, Taoist, and Native American chants.[36] Yet the inclusion of an oscillograph of the Jewish Shema and the seven candles of the menorah point to the shared Jewish-Christian tradition of the Psalter. They remind the viewer that the Psalms are prayed not only in church but in synagogue. Donald Jackson did not necessarily plan all of these connections ahead of time, but "motifs like the menorah from Matthew's Gospel just crept back in."[37] Perhaps the Holy Spirit intervened here.

The strong Jewish symbolism of the menorah throughout the Old Testament adds layers of meaning to the menorah in Matthew: the continuation of Israel, the Tree of Life, the promise to Abraham, the Jewish liturgy, and the survival of the Jewish people even through a horrific genocide committed by many claiming the name of Christ. It aesthetically establishes the Jewishness of Jesus from his birth to his death.

JESUS AND PAUL AS JEWS

Mark 5:21-43: *Two Cures*
Mark 12:29-31: *Hear, O Israel*
Deuteronomy 6:4-5: *Hear, O Israel*
Mark 1:1-12: *Baptism of Jesus*
Luke 22:14-20: *Eucharist*
Acts 9; 15; 17; 22; 25–28: *Life of Paul*

Recent scholarship on early Christianity shows plainly that it did not separate from Judaism overnight. Jesus was born and died a Jew. Paul was born a Jew, and some suggest he died a Jew as well. The National Conference of Catholic Bishops affirmed that

36. A diagram of these chants can be found in Sink, *The Art of* The Saint John's Bible, 155.
37. Calderhead, *Illuminating the Word*, 207.

Jesus was born, lived and died a Jew of his times. He, his family and all his original disciples followed the laws, traditions and customs of his people. The key concepts of Jesus' teaching, therefore, cannot be understood apart from the Jewish heritage. . . . Jesus accepted and observed the Law (cf. Gal 4:4; Lk 2:21-24), extolled respect for it, and invited obedience to it (Matt 5:17-20). Therefore, it can never be valid to place Jesus' teaching (gospel) in fundamental opposition to the Torah.[38]

Rediscovering the Jewishness of Jesus and Paul has affirmed the Jewishness of Christianity against those who would cast the two as entirely separate—the heresy of Marcion and Gnostics who cast the god of the Old Testament as completely different from the deity of the New. The process of the "parting of the ways" between these religions was protracted and continues to be strongly debated. Building on the menorah in Matthew, several Gospels illuminations in *The Saint John's Bible* reflect this ambiguity and suggest the Jewishness of Jesus and Paul.

Aidan Hart, Mark 5:21-43, *Two Cures*

Three artistic choices in *The Saint John's Bible* emphasize the Jewishness of Jesus. First, whenever Jesus or someone else speaks in Aramaic, Jackson adds the Aramaic letters in the margins or in the illumination. For example, when Mary Magdalene cries "Rabbouni!"—"My teacher!"—in John's resurrection scene, Jackson includes those letters in the illumination. Similarly, Jesus' command to the sick young woman in Mark 5:21-43 to rise, "Talitha cum!" appears in Aidan Hart's illumination to this healing scene. This use of the Hebrew alphabet, which is also the Aramaic alphabet, foregrounds the fact that Jesus was not a Greek or Roman Gentile as the church later became. He was Jewish, speaking the language of the synagogue at least occasionally.

---

38. National Conference of Catholic Bishops, *Within Context: Guidelines for the Catechetical Presentation of Jews and Judaism in the New Testament* (1986).

Second, *The Saint John's Bible* reminds the reader that Jesus' greatest commandment to "love the Lord your God" is a *Jewish* commandment. Hazel Dolby completed the text treatments to all three occurrences of this commandment in Matthew 22:37-40, Mark 12:29-31, and Luke 10:27. Dolby likewise created the text treatment for the Deuteronomy verses Jesus quotes. Dolby uses the same script, in all capital letters, for all four text treatments. While it is not a surprise that these central verses in Christianity are given special text treatments, the use of the same calligrapher and her distinctive script underscores the continuity between Torah and Christ.

Third, two Stars of David appear in crucial illuminations in the Gospels. We have already seen the Star of David in *The Call of Abraham*. The Star of David appears twice in the Gospels, first in *Baptism of Jesus*, the frontispiece to Mark. This illumination focuses not on Jesus, but on John as he walks away from the Jordan River after baptizing Jesus. In the sky above Jesus, faint golden lines make a partially formed Star of David. Imagine this as the presence of God in the scene, the voice from heaven proclaiming to Jesus, "You are my Son, the Beloved; with you I am well pleased"

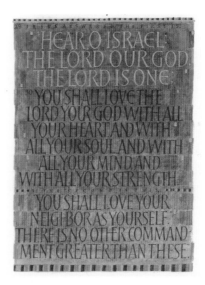

ᚼ Hazel Dolby, Mark 12:29-31: *Hear, O Israel*

ᚼ Hazel Dolby, Deuteronomy 6:4-5: *Hear, O Israel*

Donald Jackson, Mark 1:1-12: *Baptism of Jesus*

⋏ Donald Jackson, Luke 22:14-20: *Eucharist*

⋞ Donald Jackson, Mark 1:1-12: *Baptism of Jesus*, detail

(Mark 1:11). Likewise, the *Eucharist* illumination in Luke juxtaposes Stars of David and crosses to foreground the continuity of the Last Supper and the Eucharist with the Jewish Passover meal. The Committee on Illumination and Text was careful not to imply any kind of supersessionism here.[39] If "remembrance is foundational to both the Lord's supper and Passover,"[40] then both Gospel illuminations remind their viewers of Jesus' Jewishness.

Similarly, recent interpreters of Paul recognize the importance of his Jewish identity. In Romans and other letters, Paul "never suggested that the Law (Torah) had ceased to be God's will for the Jewish people."[41] Some interpreters go further, arguing that Paul did not leave Judaism on the road to Damascus, but merely became Jewish in a new way.[42] While the ecclesial documents do not state this explicitly, the Pontifical Biblical Commission affirmed in 2001 that "personally, Paul continued to be proud of his Jewish origin (Rom 11:1). . . . he continues to think and reason like a Jew,"[43] even as he sought to include Gentiles in the church.

39. For a brief discussion of the process behind this image and an early sketch, see Donald Jackson, "The Dream and the Realities," 12.

40. Amy-Jill Levine and Marc Zvi Brettler, eds., *The Jewish Annotated New Testament* (Oxford: Oxford University Press, 2011), 306, text box "Eucharist and Passover."

41. National Conference of Catholic Bishops, *Within Context* (1986).

42. For a brief presentation, see Mark D. Nanos, "Paul and Judaism," in *The Jewish Annotated New Testament* (Oxford: Oxford University Press, 2011), 551–54.

43. Pontifical Biblical Commission, *The Jewish People and Their Sacred Scriptures in the Christian Bible* (Vatican City: Libreria Editrice Vaticana, 2002), II.C.1.

Donald Jackson and Aidan Hart,
Acts 9; 15; 17; 22; 25-28:
Life of Paul

The Saint John's Bible alludes to this recent approach to Paul in *Life of Paul* in Acts. This illumination features a full-body portrait of Paul surrounded by images representing various churches, reminding the viewer of Paul's role in establishing and tending to early Christian communities. Yet even as he holds the dome to St. Peter's Cathedral in his arms, he wears a Jewish prayer shawl complete with *tallit*. One could read his holding the church while wearing the prayer shawl as an aesthetic collapse of different time periods of his life. As Calderhead explains, this shawl "evok[es] his youth as a devout Pharisee."[44] But one could also read this as an affirmation of the much-debated *continued* Jewishness of Paul.

By using these symbols associated with Judaism, *The Saint John's Bible* suggests that Jesus and Paul did not leave Judaism, but practiced it in a new way. One of these symbols, the Star of David, appears throughout Old Testament illuminations as well.

44. Calderhead, *Illuminating the Word*, 180.

THE STAR OF DAVID AND GOD'S ONGOING COVENANT WITH THE JEWS

> Genesis 15 and 17: *The Call of Abraham*
> Ruth 2:2-23: *Ruth the Gleaner*
> Judges 6 and 19: Decorative capitals

Though scholars continue to debate the historical Paul's relationship with Judaism, the Catholic Church now affirms that God's covenant with the Jews, and the Torah as the way Jews live out that covenant, are not replaced or superseded by the church's reinterpretation of that covenant. Michael Patella states that *The Saint John's Bible* "tries to emphasize the commonalities between Judaism and Christianity but without resolving all the differences."[45] The Committee on Illumination and Text was therefore concerned that the use of Jewish symbols might be interpreted not as *affirmation* of Judaism, but as an even stronger *supersessionism*, the idea that the church *replaces* the synagogue. The Scripture scholars on the Committee, Michael Patella and Irene Nowell, were "particularly attuned" to the possibility that these illuminations might be taken "as critical of Judaism."[46] Could these illuminations be taken to mean that the menorah of Matthew *replaces* the menorahs of the Old Testament?

To guard against this misreading, *The Saint John's Bible*'s inclusion of the Star of David indicates an appreciation for the *ongoing* life of Judaism. As Pope Francis affirms in his encyclical *Evangelii Gaudium*, "God continues to work among the people of the Old Covenant and to bring forth treasures of wisdom which flow from their encounter with his word."[47] It is not just the Judaism of the Old Testament or of Jesus' time that reveals something of God. It is the Judaism of Talmud, Zohar, Elie Weisel, and the communal worship of thousands of local synagogues past and present.

Unlike the Hebrew alphabet and the menorah, the Star of David is not biblical. It first appears in Jewish heraldry and folklore from medieval and early modern Europe.[48] Today, it is best known as the symbol of the state

---

45. Michael Patella, personal communication, July 10, 2017.

46. Calderhead, *Illuminating the Word*, 118.

47. Francis, *Evangelii Gaudium*: Apostolic Exhortation on the Proclamation of the Gospel in Today's World (Vatican City: Libreria Editrice Vaticana, November 24, 2013), chap. 4:IV.249.

48. Gershom Scholem, "The Star of David: History of a Symbol," in *The Messianic Idea in Judaism and Other Essays on Jewish Spirituality* (New York: Schocken, 1971), 257–81; Gerbern S. Oegema, "The Uses of the Shield of David. On Heraldic Seals and Flags, on Bible Manuscripts, Printer's Marks and Ex Libris," *Jewish Studies Quarterly*

Donald Jackson, Judges 6 and 19: Decorative capitals

of Israel. In *The Saint John's Bible*, it can be seen as symbolizing the life of Judaism after the time of Jesus.

Stars of David grace many pages of *The Saint John's Bible*'s Old Testament, beginning with Stars of David in the night sky in *The Call of Abraham*. The menorah tapestry at the end of Deuteronomy likewise contains Stars of David as the flames of the menorah. Suzanne Moore created subtle Star of David patterns in the folds of Ruth's skirt in *Ruth the Gleaner*.[49] Moore alludes to the role of the Jewish Ruth in David's genealogy, despite her being a Moabite by birth. Further, the Star of David is worked into the capitals beginning many chapters of the Pentateuch and Historical Books.[50]

With the Star of David motif established in the Old Testament, the Stars of David in Luke's *Eucharist* and Mark's *Baptism of Jesus* take on added meaning. *Eucharist* juxtaposes the Star of David with cross patterns, and *Baptism of Jesus* juxtaposes the Star of David with the double-arched doorway of the medieval St. James Cathedral at Compostela, the end of the Santiago de Compostela pilgrimage route. *Synagoga* and *ecclesia* worship side by side, as two siblings each looking toward God through different traditions and symbols.

5, no. 3 (1998): 241–53; Oegema, *History of the Shield of David: The Birth of a Symbol* (Frankfurt: Lang, 1996).

49. Calderhead, *Illuminating the Word*, 247.

50. See Gen 36; 37; 38; 40; Exod 9; Lev 6; 16; 24; Num 1; 14; 17; 29; Deut 24; 29; Josh 18; 19; Judg 6; 19; 1 Sam 15; 16; 17; 18; 26; 28; 2 Sam 3; 5; 16; 1 Kgs 12; 13; 2 Kgs 12; 13; 14; 20; 2 Chr 10; Tob 8; 1 Macc 1; 2; 3; 10; 11; 13; 2 Macc 15.

IZZY PLUDWINSKI, THE NRSV, AND COLLABORATION WITH JEWISH SCHOLARS

In *Nostra Aetate*, the Council Fathers called for Jews and Christians to study the Bible together (NA 4).[51] Subsequent Catholic teaching suggests that "Christians can learn a great deal from a Jewish exegesis practised for more than 2000 years,"[52] and that "in the field of exegesis many Jewish and Christian scholars now work together and find their collaboration mutually fruitful precisely because they belong to different religious traditions."[53] *The Saint John's Bible* responded to this call for collaboration, working with Jewish scholars and scribes in the calligraphy and the translation chosen for this Bible.

Izzy Pludwinski, a Jewish calligrapher and *sofer* (scribe) who is authorized to write Jewish sacred texts for ritual use, such as Torah scrolls, served as the Hebrew calligrapher for *The Saint John's Bible*. Pludwinski completed the Hebrew running heads on every two-page spread of the Hebrew texts in the Pentateuch, Historical Books, Wisdom Books, and Prophetic Books, and served as consultant on all Hebrew lettering.[54] As he describes it, the Hebrew lettering in the Old Testament books reminds readers that they are reading a *translation* from Hebrew, the language of the Jews. Pludwinski described his conundrum when initially asked to be on the project, quipping: "It's not a simple thing for a nice Jewish boy to write a Christian Bible." When he sought guidance, a rabbi told him: "You should do this and make it as beautiful as possible," particularly since he was only lettering for Old Testament volumes.[55] In an interview, he recounted that working on *The Saint John's Bible* was in one respect no different from any other commission, but that it was also a "spiritual game for me and [a] completely different quality" because of the collective nature of the work.[56] The collaboration was key. And so a Jewish artist's hand graces most of the pages of the Old Testament.

The Committee's choice of the New Revised Standard Version (NRSV) further echoes the contemporary collaboration between Jews and Christians

---

51. Declaration on the Relation of the Church to Non-Christian Religions (*Nostra Aetate*), October 28, 1965, 573.

52. Pontifical Biblical Commission, *Jewish People and Their Sacred Scriptures*, preface.

53. Commission for Religious Relations with the Jews, *"The Gifts and the Calling of God Are Irrevocable" (Rom 11:29)*, 7.44.

54. Sink, *The Art of* The Saint John's Bible, 372–73.

55. Calderhead, *Illuminating the Word*, 282.

56. Izzy Pludwinski, interview for *The Saint John's Bible*, YouTube, posted August 21, 2013, https://www.youtube.com/watch?v=ExyyDX_uH4U.

in biblical research. The NRSV's translation committee included Catholic, Protestant, and Orthodox scholars, and one Jewish scholar, Harry Orlinsky.[57] The NRSV is not only a standard scholarly translation but also an ecumenical and interreligious translation. Although *The Saint John's Bible* is produced by the church and indelibly stamped with its theology, that theology's inclusion of Jews and other Christians led the Committee to choose the NRSV.

As a revival of the medieval tradition of Christian illuminated Bibles, *The Saint John's Bible* reminds us that Jews never lost the tradition of writing sacred texts. A story from the creation of this Bible hints at another possible interreligious collaboration. One of the most difficult parts of planning *The Saint John's Bible* was finding a vellum supplier. In Jackson's multinational search for someone who could supply large quantities of vellum in the way he needed it, he visited a vellum supplier in Israel who supplies Jewish *soferim* like Izzy Pludwinski. Jackson later remarked, "I go to a western vellum supplier, and he says to me, 'I'm making this for cricket bat handles.' By contrast I go to Israel and here people are saying, 'In God's name, I'm asking you for this [vellum]: it will be a Torah.' It felt more comfortable, more like what I'm after."[58] Although Jackson found that the way they treated the vellum would not work for his project, this story is a tantalizing insight into what might have been: a Christian Bible written on the skin for a Torah scroll.

The production of this Bible, like its content, reflected the spirit of collaboration between Jews and Christians on biblical research post–Vatican II. What might Christians learn from Jews about writing the Word of God as an act of piety? And what might Christians learn from Jews about the shared heritage of Old Testament and Tanakh?

57. Patella, *Word and Image*, 46–47.
58. Calderhead, *Illuminating the Word*, 60.

TYPOLOGY AND THE CHRISTIAN READING OF THE OLD TESTAMENT

Isaiah 52:13–53:12: *Suffering Servant*
Genesis 15 and 17: *The Call of Abraham*
Luke 22:14-20: *Eucharist*

In a 1980 address at a synagogue, Pope John Paul II proclaimed that "the meeting between the people of God of the Old Covenant, never revoked by God, is at the same time a dialogue within our Church, that is to say, a dialogue between the first and second part of its Bible."[59] Traditionally, Christians have read the Old Testament through the lens of *typology*, looking for ways in which the Old Testament predicts or foreshadows the New. For example, Jonah is seen as a type of Christ, since he appeared to be dead and then emerged again, like Jesus who really did die and emerged from the tomb.

Without discarding the value of typology, the church's rediscovered appreciation of its Jewish heritage has led to more careful readings of the Old Testament. As Jewish New Testament scholar Amy-Jill Levine quips, the Old Testament is not *merely* a "Where's Waldo?" game of finding references to Jesus.[60] That would imply a supersessionist approach to the Old Testament, drawing on it only to validate the New without letting it speak for itself. It implies that those who have the Old Testament and not the New—the Jews—cannot gain wisdom from their Tanakh. Although Jews are not people *solely* of the Tanakh, like Christians their later traditions build on those foundational scriptures.

In response, Christians have learned to hold both the historical meaning of the Old Testament—what it meant to its original community—and its later, christological interpretation. In *The Jewish People and Their Sacred Scriptures in the Christian Bible*, the Pontifical Biblical Commission lays out an interpretive roadmap for handling this delicate issue. The document affirms that the Old Testament points to the New and the New depends on the Old, but nuances this understanding:

> It would be wrong to consider the prophecies of the Old Testament as some kind of photographic anticipations of future events. All the texts,

---

59. John Paul II, "Address at the Synagogue of Mainz" (homily, Mainz, Germany, November 17, 1980), quoted in Commission for Religious Relations with the Jews, *"The Gifts and the Calling of God Are Irrevocable" (Rom 11:29)*, 5.39.

60. Amy-Jill Levine, "The Jewish People and Their Sacred Scriptures in the Bible."

including those which later were read as messianic prophecies, already had an immediate import and meaning for their contemporaries before attaining a fuller meaning for future hearers. The messiahship of Jesus has a meaning that is new and original.[61]

Further, it clarifies that Christian rereadings of the Old Testament are *ex post facto*. Christological Old Testament readings do not merely "find" the "real" meaning that the Jews "fail" to perceive but give a new interpretation through a new lens of a Scripture that was already meaningful and valuable before Christ.[62] As such, "this new [Christological] interpretation does not negate the original meaning."[63]

While *The Saint John's Bible* frequently connects Old and New Testaments through shared symbols, it creates a *subtle* typology that does not dominate the Old Testament illuminations. Let us examine the *Suffering Servant* of Isaiah as a case study.

Suffering Servant treats an Old Testament passage frequently read christologically, the Suffering Servant in Isaiah. The fourth of Isaiah's Servant Songs, this passage speaks of the trials undergone by a Servant of God, "despised and rejected by others; a man of suffering and acquainted with infirmity" (Isa 53:3a). This Servant bears the misdeeds of his fellow humans, for which God will reward him (Isa 53:10-12). The identity of this Suffering Servant remains mysterious. Jewish traditions variously read the Servant as Israel, a minority within Israel, the Messiah, Jeremiah, or Moses.[64] The New Testament writers applied the image of the Suffering Servant to Jesus, building on pre-Christian Jewish interpretation that saw the Servant as the coming Messiah.[65] New Testament scholar Ben Witherington, in his book on Christian typology and Isaiah, typifies the complexities of current Christian interpretation of this prophetic book. While holding that the historical

---

61. Pontifical Biblical Commission, *Jewish People and Their Sacred Scriptures* II.A.4.

62. Ibid., II.A.6.

63. Ibid., II.A.2.

64. Berlin and Brettler, *The Jewish Study Bible*.

65. See various essays in Bernd Janowski and Peter Stuhlmacher, eds., *The Suffering Servant: Isaiah 53 in Jewish and Christian Sources*, trans. Daniel P. Bailey (Grand Rapids, MI: Eerdmans, 2004); especially Martin Hengel, "The Effective History of Isaiah 53 in the Pre-Christian Period," in *The Suffering Servant: Isaiah 53 in Jewish and Christian Sources*, ed. Bernd Janowski and Peter Stuhlmacher, trans. Daniel P. Bailey (Grand Rapids, MI: Eerdmans, 2004), 75–146.

Jesus is the clearest instantiation of the Suffering Servant,[66] he still insists that "the first task of any good interpreter of the Bible is to hear the text in its original historical contexts to the best of our ability before we turn to the later use and reaudiencing and reapplying of the material by the [New Testament] writers."[67]

Jackson *could have* illuminated the Suffering Servant with a clear iconographic reference to Jesus. He could have made the Suffering Servant a bright golden figure, echoing his depiction of Jesus in *Word Made Flesh* or other Gospels illuminations, or asked Aidan Hart to create a face or body evoking Hart's Gospels illuminations of Jesus. This would have made the typological interpretation too strong, however, eclipsing Isaiah's historical, literal sense. Jackson could have also erased all possibility of christological reference in this illumination, a danger warned against by the Pontifical Biblical Commission.[68] Instead, the Committee and Jackson produced an image that masterfully works on both literal and christological levels.

On the literal level, Jackson relates the Suffering Servant to contemporary examples of people undergoing persecution and suffering at the hands of their fellow humans. His Servant is a starving African child, a condemnation of the greed and corruption of humanity that allows people to die of hunger on a planet where we have enough food to feed everyone. The child stands in the Gate of No Return at Elmina Castle in Ghana, through which enslaved people were forced to board boats bound for the New World. Superimposed on the entire image are chain-link fence patterns taken from photos of the American prison at Guantanamo Bay, where many prisoners are either known to be innocent or have been given no due process of law.

Yet a closer look at the image reveals a christological level of meaning as well. The image is shaped like a cross.[69] The gold bars above the Gate of No Return seem to allude to the square cross motifs in Gospels and Acts, though their lack of shining illumination reflects the seeming absence of God in the Servant's pains. The ram's head at the bottom of the illumination, comparing the Suffering Servant to a sacrificial lamb (Isa 53:7), also appears in *Eucharist*, creating a typological link between the two: the Suffering Servant led like a lamb to sacrifice is Jesus led to the cross. In *The Call of Abraham*, the ram's head refers most directly to the binding of Isaac. Like Isaiah's Suffering

---

66. Ben Witherington III, *Isaiah Old and New: Exegesis, Intertextuality, and Hermeneutics* (Minneapolis, MN: Fortress Press, 2017), 248.

67. Ibid., 9.

68. Pontifical Biblical Commission, *Jewish People and Their Sacred Scriptures* II.A.4.

69. I am indebted to Leah Machinskas-Le for this observation.

Servant, Isaac is a precursor of Christ. Yet in both *The Call of Abraham* and *Suffering Servant*, a typological reading is subtle and only one layer of meaning in a multifaceted piece of art. The typology becomes clearer in the light of the New Testament—in this case, Luke's *Eucharist*. The creators of *The Saint John's Bible* were attuned to the complexities of christological readings of the Old Testament. For Christians, the Old Testament must be read in the light of the New. But it must also speak directly to us on its own terms.

Donald Jackson, Isaiah 52:13–53:12: *Suffering Servant*

BEYOND JEWISH-CHRISTIAN DIALOGUE?

This chapter began with the frontispiece to Matthew, with its references to Buddhism and Islam as well as Judaism. So why have we focused solely on Judaism? Although *The Saint John's Bible* makes occasional reference to other religions—the oscillographs of the Psalms frontispiece come to mind—it primarily focuses on Judaism. This focus reminds the viewer that this is primarily a *Catholic* Bible. As one member of the Committee stated, "How worldwide do we want to be? How Catholic? It brought up issues for us—what about Buddhist images? This is a Catholic Bible for a Catholic community. The images have to fit that."[70] The Jewish imagery in *The Saint John's Bible* is not just some kind of trendy interreligious outreach, but a thoughtful and powerful expression of Christianity's close ties with Judaism through its Scripture: "The dialogue with Judaism is for Christians something quite special, since Christianity possesses Jewish roots which determine relations between the two in a unique way."[71] Christian-Jewish relations are unlike Christian relations with any other religion, because Christianity comes out of Judaism and retains its core sacred texts.

Catholics, however, are not the only ones whose ethical imaginations are stirred by this Bible. As *The Saint John's Bible* ambassador Jason Paul Engel, OblSB, found when showing the Historical Books to a group of Jewish women, "A couple of women started crying. One told me 'We can't believe that Christians would treat our scripture with such reverence and beauty.' "[72] Though undoubtedly a Bible of the church, *The Saint John's Bible* is also a gift to all humanity. Like Paul's rebuke to the Gentile Christians of Rome not to "boast over the branches" (Rom 11:18), *The Saint John's Bible* grafts the olive tree of faith back together to create a harmonious family—a fitting symbol, given that the olive branch traditionally symbolizes peace.[73]

We began this chapter with Matthew's menorah, which includes the names of the women in Jesus' family line. This illumination also contains the image of the mandala, which appears in *Garden of Eden*. This feminine presence continues in the menorahs in Genesis and Deuteronomy and Ruth, which look like tapestries sewn by women. It is to the topic of women in *The Saint John's Bible* and feminist biblical interpretation that we now turn.

70. Calderhead, *Illuminating the Word*.

71. Commission for Religious Relations with the Jews, *"The Gifts and the Calling of God Are Irrevocable" (Rom 11:29)*, 2.14.

72. Jason Paul Engel, personal communication, May 24, 2017.

73. Ferguson, *Signs and Symbols in Christian Art*, 35.

Chapter Three

TREE OF KNOWLEDGE, TREE OF LIFE
Women and Wisdom Women

Caroline Mackenzie, *The Creator* (2013)

Following in the footsteps of the Samaritan woman and Mary Magdalene in John's gospel, women have read the Bible and preached Christ through the lens of their female experiences since Jesus' earthly life. British Christian artist Caroline Mackenzie envisions a feminine image of God in her bronze sculpture *The Creator.*

Mackenzie's female personification of Wisdom holds a hammer and chisel, since she "was beside him, like a master worker" (Prov 8:30) at creation.[1] Mackenzie explains that her work emerges from an engagement with Hindu art, which "link[s] female humanity with the divine"[2] by using both feminine and masculine incarnations of deities. Mackenzie's *The Creator* might also be a self-portrait of a

1. Grace Ji-Sun Kim, "Made in the Image of God: Art, Feminist Theology and Caroline Mackenzie," *Huffington Post*, March 7, 2015, http://www.huffingtonpost.com/grace-jisun-kim/made-in-the-image-of-god-_1_b_6807964.html.

2. Caroline Mackenzie, "Intro," *Caroline Mackenzie*, http://carolinemackenzie.co.uk/creative-women/.

woman artist who, in creating sculpture with tools like a hammer and chisel, herself embodies the creative spirit of Woman Wisdom.

Mackenzie's work reminds us that Christian feminists express their faith not only through biblical scholarship but also through unleashing their creative imaginations to make theater, storytelling, midrash, music, art, and dance to envision a world that affirms the equality and dignity of all humanity.[3] They focus on the "prophetic and liberating elements" of Christianity with "attention to the neglect of women's full incorporation into the people of God."[4] In recent decades, Christian feminists have struggled with issues from feminine language for God, to empowering women as clergy, to critiquing patriarchal and sexist elements of Christianity.

Catholic feminist biblical interpretation, one strand of Christian feminism, has born fruits among scholars and laypeople for the past forty years. It has been given new life in the Wisdom Bible Commentary, a multivolume feminist commentary on every book of the Bible, edited by New Testament scholar Barbara Reid, OP.

While feminist biblical interpretation has at times been viewed with suspicion by the magisterium, the Pontifical Biblical Commission's on *The Interpretation of the Bible in the Church* concedes that "feminine sensitivity helps to unmask and correct certain commonly accepted interpretations which were tendentious and sought to justify the male domination of women."[5] While the Commission cautions against forms of feminism that "den[y] all authority to the Bible," they accept forms of feminism that offer prophetic service to the church.

The Saint John's Bible emphasizes key biblical women, often foregrounding their experience and their witness. Other times, it inserts women where they may not be explicit in the narrative. The key symbols for women in the art of *The Saint John's Bible* are bright, colorful fabric patterns and shining silver. Jackson remarks that "textiles are deeply symbolic of interconnectivity. Interweaving threads join to make a wonderful whole."[6] The choice of textiles to symbolize the feminine reflects the importance of women in creating textiles in ancient Israel and the importance of women in many cultures for weaving together families and communities.[7] Silver alludes to

3. Barbara E. Reid, *Wisdom's Feast: An Invitation to Feminist Interpretation of the Scriptures* (Grand Rapids, MI: Eerdmans, 2016), 10; Elisabeth Schüssler Fiorenza, *Wisdom Ways: Introducing Feminist Biblical Interpretation* (Maryknoll, NY: Orbis Books, 2001), 179–83.

4. Anne M. Clifford, *Introducing Feminist Theology* (Maryknoll, NY: Orbis Books, 2000), 28–29.

5. Pontifical Biblical Commission, *Interpretation of the Bible* I.E.2.

6. Calderhead, *Illuminating the Word*, 98.

7. Carol Meyers, *Rediscovering Eve: Ancient Israelite Women in Context* (Oxford: Oxford University Press, 2012), 133.

the moon and Woman Wisdom. Our story of women in this Bible begins and ends with trees: the Tree of Knowledge in the Garden of Eden and the Tree of Life in the Wisdom Books.

EVE AND THE SERPENT

Genesis 1:1–2:3: *Creation*
Genesis 2:4-25: *Adam and Eve*
Genesis 3:1-24: *Garden of Eden*

The figure of Eve in Genesis 1–3 is crucial in many Christian formulations of gender and womanhood, whether denigrating Eve as "weak and fickle"[8] or celebrating her as "the curious one, the seeker of knowledge, the tester of limits."[9] These widely different interpretations result from the ambiguity of Eve in Genesis itself, an ambiguity recreated in Jackson's *Adam and Eve*.

Modern historical critics separate the first creation story (Gen 1:1–2:3) from the second (Gen 2:4-25). Feminist exegetes have frequently noted that the first creation story does not establish any gender hierarchy, unlike the second one, in which Eve is fashioned from Adam's side. In illuminating Genesis 1:1–2:3, the Committee intended to foreground gender equality, as God created both male and female in Her image: "humankind is first created as a species and then differentiated between male and female."[10] In the illumination of the first creation story, *Creation*, the sixth day—the sixth column in the image—displays both male and female in prehistoric cave paintings. The figure at the bottom of the column, who appears to be female, is intertwined with the image of the coral snake, alluding to what is to come in the Garden. But the image's inclusion of both genders reminds the viewer that both male *and* female are made in the image of God.

The story of Adam and Eve's eviction from the garden (Gen 3) frequently appears in arguments about the character of womankind. In one traditional Western Christian reading from Augustine onward, this expulsion represents humanity's archetypal rebellion against God. Eve gets the blame for this loss of divine intimacy because she eats of the forbidden fruit first. Thus,

8. Reid, *Wisdom's Feast*, 26, quoting John Chrysostom.
9. Susan Niditch, "Genesis," in *Women's Bible Commentary*, ed. Carol A. Newsom, Sharon H. Ringe, and Jacqueline E. Lapsley, 3rd ed. (Louisville, KY: Westminster John Knox, 2012), 31.
10. Patella, *Word and Image*, 87.

she becomes the seductress responsible for the downfall of humanity. More recent feminist scholars, however, have tried to rehabilitate Eve. They point out that Adam did not object to Eve's eating from the Tree of Knowledge of Good and Evil, nor did he refuse to follow in her path. While Adam is passive and silent, Eve is "knowledgeable, articulate, and well-informed about God's command. . . . Contrary to contemporary gender stereotypes, the woman is the vocal and active agent, the man is passive and acquiescent."[11] Rather than the worst mistake in human history, perhaps the supposed "Fall" was merely a necessary step in the development of human independence and ability to know good and evil—and therefore to *truly* choose good. If eating the fruit is a good thing, then Eve should be commended for her initiative. If God did not want Adam and Eve to eat from the tree, why would God place the tree in the garden? Is Eve a Promethean culture hero or a contemptible temptress?

Donald Jackson,
Genesis 2:4-25: *Adam and Eve*

At first glance, *The Saint John's Bible* reflects the traditional account of Eve as temptress. The illumination depicts Eve behind Adam surrounded by bright textile borders. *The Saint John's Bible* uses textiles to symbolize feminine presence, hinting that Eve is the center of this story. Eve, whose face is in color and has more light, grins at a shadowy and grim Adam. Adam looks dead, indicating perhaps an inner spiritual death. The coral snake seems to have taken over Eve entirely: wraps around her neck, jewelry, and hair, comes out of her mouth, and forms her eyebrows. Donald Jackson's choice of the beautiful yet highly poisonous coral snake to illuminate the serpent in the garden suggests that he may not read the serpent as a good figure, or Eve's choice as a good one.[12] Rather, she has brought poison into the world. Adam and Eve do not make eye contact, symbolizing the loss of their emotional and spiritual contact. The gold in this work is *not* illuminated because God's presence is lost after the expulsion from the Garden.

Yet the snake imagery and Eve's smile remain ambiguous. Eve *may* wear a malicious grin.

11. Reid, *Wisdom's Feast*, 28.
12. Patella, *Word and Image*, 90.

Jackson calls her "a deliciously mischievous girl."[13] It is also possible, however, to see her grin as the joy of one who has found knowledge, who has
discovered the difference between good and evil. This image may capture
the moment after Eve partook of the forbidden fruit but before Adam did
so. Thus his grey face would be not the result of any fall, but the dullness
of one who has not yet become a full human, a mock-up model of the final
product. After all, what is more quintessentially
human than an understanding of good and evil—a
conscience? The previous illumination, *Garden of
Eden*, hints at this possibility by including a patch
of the mandala pattern from *Genealogy of Jesus*
and *Luke Anthology*.

Adam and Eve's eating from the tree is often
deemed a *felix culpa*, a happy fault, because it led
to the coming of Christ to reverse the Fall. In a
typological reading of this illumination, perhaps
Eve is smiling because she knows what her action
will lead to: the coming of Jesus, whose parables
continue to unveil the knowledge of good and evil.

In the right-hand margin of this illumination
appears a quote from 2 Corinthians 3:18: "And all
of us, with unveiled faces, seeing the glory of the
Lord as though reflected in a mirror, are being
transformed into the same image from one degree
of glory to another." This quotation works at multiple levels. Jackson remarks that "behind Eve is a
platinum background, like a mirror, to refer to the
quotation. . . . Eve and Adam are mirrors of us."[14]
In the context of 2 Corinthians 3, the veiling Paul
mentions refers to the veil Moses puts over his face
because he cannot look at the face of God, but also
to the veil over the understanding of those who
did not accept Christ. Adam and Eve experience
an unveiled closeness with God—at least until they
veil themselves from God by hiding after eating
the forbidden fruit (Gen 3:8).

13. Calderhead, *Illuminating the Word*, 191.
14. Ibid.

Donald Jackson and Chris Tomlin,
Genesis 3:1-24: *Garden of Eden*

In the context of a Bible full of images, a quotation about *seeing* the glory of the Lord and the image of God evokes the power of art to inspire beatific vision. In the context of *The Saint John's Bible*, the image of the glory of the Lord reflected in a mirror points forward to Woman Wisdom. We can also see Eve as the first of many powerful women in the Bible.

COURAGEOUS WOMEN OF THE OLD TESTAMENT

Judges 4–5: *Deborah Anthology*
Esther 5:1-14: *Esther*
Ruth 1:1-22: *Ruth and Naomi*
Ruth 2:2-23: *Ruth the Gleaner*
2 Kings 22:1-20: *Huldah the Prophetess*

Biblical women are often stereotyped as meek, mild, and exclusively maternal. Despite the focus on men's deeds in the Bible and the frequent childbirth necessary for cultural survival in the ancient world, which kept women mainly in the domestic sphere,[15] several women in the Old Testament transgressed their expected roles at pivotal moments to deliver their people from distress. *The Saint John's Bible* highlights the valor and value of these women for today.

Judges 4–5 gives us two stories of powerful women: Deborah, who was judge over Israel, and Jael, who delivered Israel from war with Canaan. Jael defeats a man precisely *because* he assumes a mere woman would not attack him. Sisera, a Canaanite leader, was leading a war against Israel when he stopped in Jael's tent for some refreshment. After serving him some milk and lulling him to sleep, Jael drives a tent peg through his temple. Gruesome as this sounds, it becomes less so when the author of Judges hints that he raped women taken in war (Judg 5:30).[16]

15. Meyers, *Rediscovering Eve.*

16. Alice Ogden Bellis, *Helpmates, Harlots, and Heroes: Women's Stories in the Hebrew Bible*, 2nd ed. (Louisville, KY: Westminster John Knox, 2007), 107.

Donald Jackson, Judges 4–5: *Deborah Anthology*

The illumination is delightfully ambiguous: Who is the woman in the image? Patella labels her as Deborah because of her stately, regal attire, while Sink marks her as Jael because she is holding the tent peg.[17] Perhaps Jackson intended this image to represent them both. Certainly the fearsome face of the woman in this image could represent either Deborah or Jael. Deborah and, to a lesser extent, Jael have been at the center of disputes among Jews and Christians about women holding leadership roles.[18]

The Saint John's Bible highlights the figure of Esther as a woman who wields great power and courage in saving the people of Israel, but undergoes significant personal trauma to do so. In the book telling her story, Esther is a young Jewish woman who becomes queen of Persia by winning the king Ahasuerus over with her charm and beauty. (Ahasuerus demoted his previous queen, Vashti, because she would not display her beauty to his drunken friends.) After averting an attempted genocide of her people, Esther leads the Jews in a slaughter of thousands of Persians.

Feminist exegetes are divided on Esther. Some favor Vashti, who refused to support the king's demeaning demand at great personal cost, over Esther who, they allege, played into the patriarchal system: "For many women, Vashti is the more palatable female character, since she directly challenges the status quo."[19] Yet other feminist interpreters have turned to Esther as an example of a woman who did what she *had* to do. Angeline M.G. Song terms this the "pragmatism of the powerless," the ability to survive and thrive in a hostile system by playing its games to subtly empower oneself.[20] She focuses on both the trauma and the power dynamics of Esther's story as a window on today.

Jackson's *Esther* highlights her trauma as she navigates the power dynamics of her situation. Esther's face is divided down the middle, indicating the difficulty of her double life as both queen in the palace and subjugated Jew in diaspora. Like Deborah-Jael, her monarchical side sports a

17. Patella, *Word and Image*, 113–14; Sink, *The Art of* The Saint John's Bible, 41–42.

18. Anne W. Stewart, "Deborah, Jael, and Their Interpreters," in *Women's Bible Commentary*, ed. Carol A. Newsom, Sharon H. Ringe, and Jacqueline E. Lapsley, 3rd ed. (Louisville, KY: Westminster John Knox, 2012), 130.

19. Sidnie White Crawford, "Esther," in *Women's Bible Commentary*, ed. Carol A. Newsom, Sharon H. Ringe, and Jacqueline E. Lapsley, 3rd ed. (Louisville, KY: Westminster John Knox, 2012), 203.

20. Angeline Song, "Heartless Bimbo or Subversive Role Model? A Narrative (Self) Critical Reading of the Character of Esther," *Dialog* 49, no. 1 (2010): 60.

that I will prepare for them, and then I will do as the king has said." ¶ Haman went out that day happy and in good spirits. But when Haman saw Mordecai in the king's gate, and observed that he neither rose nor trembled before him, he was infuriated with Mordecai; "nevertheless Haman restrained himself and went home. Then he sent & called for his friends & his wife Zeresh." and Haman recounted to them the splendor of his riches, the number of his sons, all the promotions with which the king had honored him, and how he had advanced him above the officials and the ministers of the king." Haman added, "Even Queen Esther let no one but myself come with the king to the banquet that she prepared. Tomorrow also I am invited by her, together with the king.

Donald Jackson, Esther 5:1-14: *Esther*

rich headdress made up of elements from Persian and Palestinian adornments.[21] She looks made-up in two senses of the word: she wears the cosmetics and jewelry of a queen, and she is disguising her true self. The look on her queenly face is reminiscent of a model in a catalog, the kind of sultry "come hither" look some women wear as a mask to attract men. But on her Jewish side, the same facial expression appears shadowy, as if she has donned ashes alongside the rest of her people facing their pogrom (Esth 4:1- 3). The text of Esther 14:15 and 14:19 below her further highlight her ambivalence about the royal garments she must don. Jackson based this illumination on Gustav Klimt's *Judith and the Head of Holofernes* (1901), a portrait of Adele Bloch-Bauer, his patroness who was married to a wealthy older man— like Esther, a woman who uses her sexuality as a form of power in a world of limited options.[22] *The Saint John's Bible* highlights the trauma of Esther's sexual servitude and the pain of colonization, but it also celebrates Esther's intelligence and ingenuity in hiding her identity to save her people.

Esther, a woman of Israel, ascends to the palace of a foreign people. Ruth does the opposite. A Moabite by birth, she becomes an Israelite, an ancestor of David, and a prototype for Jewish converts to this day. The book of Ruth, though one of the shortest books in the Old Testament, has *three* illuminations: Donald Jackson's *Ruth Genealogy* and Suzanne Moore's *Ruth and Naomi* and *Ruth the Gleaner*. Moore's pieces focus on Ruth and her relationship with Naomi. Their bond exemplifies an uncommon phenomenon in the Bible: a nuanced portrait of a close bond between two women. Ruth's bold proposal to Boaz on behalf of Naomi testifies to Ruth's courage and loyalty.

21. Patella, *Word and Image*, 147.
22. Sink, *The Art of* The Saint John's Bible, 93.

The first illumination, *Ruth and Naomi*, reflects their friendship. They stand or sit next to each other, reminiscent of Mary and Martha's posture in *Jesus with Mary and Martha* in Luke. Here they embrace as they look forward with fear and faith as widows. Above their heads Moore inserts geometric patterns, "a reflection of mathematical principles and proportions found in nature . . . to suggest a sort of cosmic order to the universe."[23] Even as Ruth and Naomi might not see how their fate will turn out, God has a plan for them. Moore emphasizes their commonality in their similar appearance: "who can say which one is the foreigner?"[24]

On the next page, Moore's portrait of Ruth gleaning in the field looks back to *Ruth and Naomi*. She is thinking about her mother-in-law while she is in the fields. Her head is upright, proud, brave. At the illumination's center is a circular vortex: a bundle of wheat in Ruth's cloak, alluding to the agricultural plenty that Ruth and Naomi found in Bethlehem "at the beginning of the barley harvest" (Ruth 1:22), in contrast to the famine in Moab where the story of Ruth begins. The bundle may also be Ruth's womb pregnant with Obed, or the cosmos itself. Ruth's skirt dances as she moves through the field gleaning, perhaps a joyful dance like that of Woman Wisdom in Moore's *Praise of Wisdom*.

Women were not only judges and converts in ancient Israel but also prophets. One such prophet, Huldah (2 Kgs 22:1-20), receives a full illumination hinting at the contributions of women to a Bible written most likely entirely by men. During

23. Ibid., 54.
24. Ibid., 55.

Suzanne Moore,
Ruth 1:1-22: *Ruth and Naomi*

Suzanne Moore,
Ruth 2:2-23: *Ruth the Gleaner*

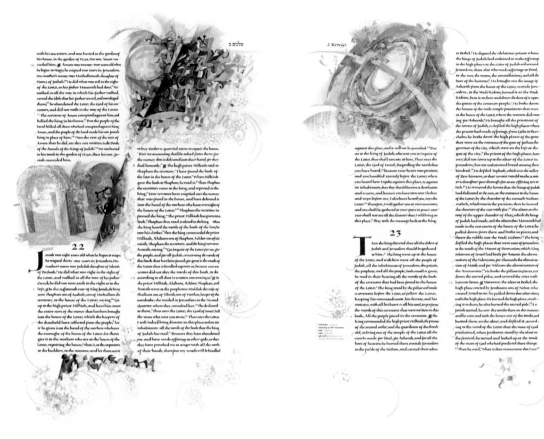

Suzanne Moore, 2 Kings 22:1-20: *Huldah the Prophetess*

the reign of Josiah, the high priest Hilkiah finds a book of laws in the sanctuary. Josiah consults Huldah the prophetess about what God is planning to do. Huldah gives Josiah a pessimistic prognosis: Judah will be conquered and taken into foreign captivity in Babylon, but Josiah will not live to see it. Although her advice launched "sweeping religious reforms," she may have been relatively independent from the temple.[25] The officials go to her *home* to consult her, hinting that she is distinct from the prophets at the royal-religious complex. Although the author of 2 Kings gives us only a brief passage about this prophetess, "it is intriguing to wonder whether Huldah may

25. Cameron B. R. Howard, "1 and 2 Kings," in *Women's Bible Commentary*, ed. Carol A. Newsom, Sharon H. Ringe, and Jacqueline E. Lapsley, 3rd ed. (Louisville, KY: Westminster John Knox, 2012), 178.

have prophesied much more than this one instance and whether many of her words have been lost to us. We wish that a book of Huldah had survived."[26] Huldah is a reminder that there were more prophets in ancient Israel than only those whose words made their way into the Bible.

Moore's *Huldah the Prophetess* follows up on this suggestion. The illumination is divided in two pages. On the first page, a double-arched doorway taken from Huldah's gate at the Temple Mount in Jerusalem represents temple and royal court—the institutions of Hilkiah and Josiah.[27] Moore explains that double doors also represent heaven (left) and infinity (right).[28] Separated from the temple doors is a whirling vortex with words pouring forth. Sink writes, "The primary image is that of a quill, from which unrolls an image of a scroll."[29] Moore borrowed letters from sacred texts in several languages, including the Dead Sea Scrolls and the Cherokee alphabet.[30] The words spilling out onto the page emanate more from Huldah's realm than from Hilkiah's. On the next page, a large vortex pattern symbolizes a rolled scroll, but also the chaos of prophetic power and the cosmos.[31] If the scroll represents the preservation of law and history, then the image hints at Huldah's role behind these traditions as we know them today. What role did women play in the development of the oral and written traditions that made their way into the Old Testament? Even if no woman wrote down the words of the Bible, were their oral traditions written down and copied by male scribes?

Moore deliberately connects the cosmic vortex of *Huldah the Prophetess* with Ruth's womb in *Ruth the Gleaner*, also alluding to other cosmic imagery such as *To the Ends of the Earth* in Acts.[32] The womb gives new life to individuals just as God's creation of the cosmos gives new life to humanity. The wheat stalks emerging from Ruth's basket look like the bird feathers used to make quills to write *The Saint John's Bible*, the quill also in *Huldah the Prophetess*. If the scroll of Huldah is also the womb of Ruth, then we might

---

26. Bellis, *Helpmates, Harlots, and Heroes*, 154.

27. Sink, *The Art of* The Saint John's Bible, 86.

28. Suzanne Moore, personal communication, July 7, 2017.

29. Sink, *The Art of* The Saint John's Bible, 85–86.

30. Prior to her work on *The Saint John's Bible*, Moore spent several years exploring the Cherokee script through calligraphy. See Suzanne Moore, *Painted Speech: A Written Celebration of Sequoyah's Cherokee Alphabet* (Ashfield, MA: Suzanne Moore, 1988), and *Tracing Magic Lines: 4 Tributes to Sequoyah and the Cherokee Syllabary* (Ashfield, MA: Suzanne Moore, 1990).

31. Patella, *Word and Image*, 143; Suzanne Moore, personal communication, July 7, 2017.

32. Suzanne Moore, personal communication, July 7, 2017.

think of Ruth's womb as another biblical author: without Ruth there would be no line of descent to Jesus, thus no New Testament.

In the Pontifical Biblical Commission's 1977 document analyzing the possibility of women becoming priests, the Commission notes the presence of these exemplary women in the Bible:

> There are women who bore the name of prophetess (Maria, Deborah, Huldah, Noiada), while not playing the role of the great prophets. Other women exercised an important function for the salvation of the people of God at critical moments of this people's history (for example, Judith, Esther).[33]

These women point to the fact that women were *not* always in the background, the stage crew in a world dominated by the theater of men. At times they came forward with a pivotal role in Israel's male-dominated political and military spheres. *The Saint John's Bible* does these women justice by highlighting and magnifying their presence and power.

WOMEN IN THE BIRTH AND MINISTRY OF JESUS

Luke 2:1-14: *Birth of Christ*
Luke 1:46-55: *Magnificat*
Jeremiah 1:1-10: *Now the Word*
John 11:1-44: *Raising of Lazarus*
Luke 10; 15; 16: *Luke Anthology* and *Jesus with Mary and Martha*

Just as *The Saint John's Bible* highlights the role of women at pivotal moments in ancient Israel, it also highlights pivotal women in the life of Jesus, from before his birth to after his resurrection. By focusing on the experiences of these women and their witness, *The Saint John's Bible* engages in the remembering of women's witness crucial for feminist biblical interpretation.

This remembering begins with the women important in Jesus' life even before his birth. On the very first page of *Gospels and Acts*, *Genealogy of Jesus*, the frontispiece to Matthew, displays Jesus' family tree as a menorah. While Matthew mentions only five women in the genealogy, Jackson incorporates *all* the women in his illumination, finding their names scattered throughout the Old Testament. The five women named in the genealogy do not paint a picture of Jesus' perfect, priestly pedigree. Rahab the Canaanite and Ruth the Moabite are foreigners. Bathsheba and Tamar conceived their sons out of wedlock.

---

33. Pontifical Biblical Commission, "Can Women Be Priests?," *Origins* 6 (July 1, 1976), 92–96.

Donald Jackson,
Luke 2:1-14: *Birth of Christ*

Mary became pregnant while still betrothed, as "the divine family plan moves in ways that contravene traditional family values."[34] Jackson's choice to include *all* women—even Hagar—signals a strong feminist reading of Matthew's genealogy, even as it lessens Matthew's focus on outsiders and the marginalized.[35]

In one subtle symbolic connection, Jackson emphasizes the miracle of maternity in the birth of Jesus. In *Birth of Christ*, the frontispiece to Luke, Jackson supplies the only illumination of Jesus' mother Mary in *The Saint John's Bible*. Here, she leans joyfully over the manger, with its Jesus absent because *we* are to place him there in our own lives.[36] On the next page, Mary's *Magnificat* is augmented with a special text treatment in radiant gold.

34. Amy-Jill Levine, "Gospel of Matthew," in *Women's Bible Commentary*, ed. Carol A. Newsom, Sharon H. Ringe, and Jacqueline E. Lapsley, 3rd ed. (Louisville, KY: Westminster John Knox, 2012), 467.

35. Fraher, "The Illuminated Imagination: Layered Metaphor in *The Saint John's Bible* Frontispiece *Genealogy of Christ*," 13.

36. Patella, *Word and Image*, 247.

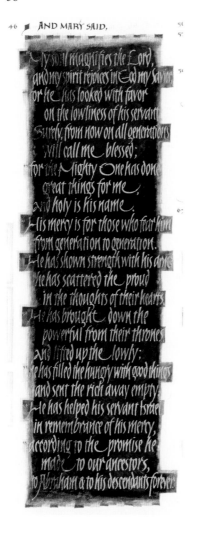

◁ Sally Mae Joseph,
Luke 1:46-55:
Magnificat

▷ Sally Mae Joseph,
Jeremiah 1:1-10,
Now the Word

The *Magnificat* is central not only to Catholic devotion and liturgy but also to feminist biblical interpreters who deem it "the great New Testament song of liberation . . . a revolutionary document of intense conflict and victory,"[37] and from it argue that Mary is a prophet.[38] *The Saint John's Bible* connects Mary with the Old Testament prophetic tradition by using the same script and chrysography—gold letters—to write God's words calling Jeremiah to prophesy.

37. Jane D. Schaberg and Sharon H. Ringe, "Gospel of Luke," in *Women's Bible Commentary*, ed. Carol A. Newsom, Sharon H. Ringe, and Jacqueline E. Lapsley, 3rd ed. (Louisville, KY: Westminster John Knox, 2012), 504.

38. N. Clayton Croy and Alice E. Connor, "Mantic Mary? The Virgin Mother as Prophet in Luke 1.26-56 and the Early Church," *Journal for the Study of the New Testament* 34, no. 3 (2012): 254–76.

me;²⁶ but you do not believe, because you do not belong to my sheep.²⁷ My sheep hear my voice. I know them, and they follow me.²⁸ I give them eternal life, and they will never perish. No one will snatch them out of my hand.²⁹ What my Father has given me is greater than all else, and no one can snatch it out of the Father's hand.³⁰ The Father and I are one." ³¹ The Jews took up stones again to stone him.³² Jesus replied,"I have shown you many good works from the Father. For which of these are you going to stone me?³³ The Jews answered,"It is not for a good work

I AM THE RESURRECTION AND THE LIFE

Donald Jackson, John 11:1-44: *Raising of Lazarus*

Just as Jeremiah is consecrated to be a prophet while in the womb, so Mary serves as a prophet while Jesus is in *her* womb, and likewise the fetal Jesus is called to be a prophet before his birth. Both the background of *Magnificat* and Mary's cloak in *Birth of Christ* are in the royal blue traditionally associated with Mary—though supplemented in *Birth of Christ* by Mary's bold red shirt under her cloak.[39]

As the border to *Birth of Christ*, Jackson employs a textile pattern used only also in *Raising of Lazarus*. In this illumination, the viewer looks from the perspective of Lazarus inside the tomb, rather than the crowd outside the tomb. We are Lazarus, seeking resurrection.

Lazarus sits up and moves toward the light at the end of the tunnel, symbolizing Jackson's mother's near-death experience when giving birth to him.[40] By connecting his own birth with Lazarus' new life, Jackson links Jesus' miracle of raising Lazarus with the miracle of new life worked through women worldwide. The connection between Lazarus' rebirth and women's childbirth also evokes Lazarus' sisters Mary and Martha, who place faith in

39. Ferguson, *Signs and Symbols in Christian Art*, 151; Laura Kelly Fanucci, "Variation on a Theme: Intertextuality in the Illuminations of the Gospel of Luke," *Obsculta* 2, no. 1 (2009): 23. Thanks to Anne Kaese for pointing out the significance of Mary's red shirt.

40. Patella, *Word and Image*, 264.

Donald Jackson and Aidan Hart, Luke 10; 15; 16:
Luke Anthology

Donald Jackson, Luke 10; 15; 16:
Jesus with Mary and Martha

Jesus by appealing to him for a miracle in saving their brother (John 11:3). Mary was not just a random vessel. Her faith and witness, demonstrated by her canticle and her courage in bearing a baby despite social stigma, make her a prophet and miracle worker in her own right.

In Jesus' ministry, women such as Mary and Martha performed crucial roles as witnesses to and disciples of Jesus. The *Luke Anthology* illuminates several parables from Luke. From top to bottom, the parables are the Lost Coin (Luke 15:8-10), the Lost Sheep (Luke 15:4-7), the Good Samaritan (Luke 10:29-37), the Prodigal Son (Luke 15:11-32), and Lazarus and the Rich Man (Luke 16:19-31). The parables are illuminated in diagonal strips running up to a pure golden Jesus at top right. Mary and Martha are below

Jesus, listening, in the audience when Jesus tells some of the parables in this illumination (Luke 10:38-42). Their familial, friendly posture alludes to *Ruth and Naomi.*

Jesus' words to Martha are often used to justify the exclusion of women from leadership positions in the church, for Mary has chosen the better part: silently listening to the teachings of Jesus, in contrast to Martha's service, her *diakonia.*[41] Many modern women, however, struggling to balance the demands of work and family while still carving out time for prayer, find themselves identifying with Martha.[42]

Rather than esteeming one over the other, *The Saint John's Bible* values *both* Mary's contemplation and Martha's service.[43] Jackson depicts Mary on the left, sitting in contemplation, while Martha on the right stands with her hands on her hips as if she has paused from walking. The textile pattern to her right, with circles containing crosses that look like eucharistic bread, reminds us that Mary is not just tidying up while ignoring the priceless teaching spoken in her home. She is like the members of many churches' altar guilds, who set up the bread and the wine in the sacristy before each service. Their work remains unseen by the community at large, but is necessary for the Eucharist to take place. Luke refers to Martha's service as *diakonia,* a word used elsewhere in the New Testament to refer to setting a table for a meal and, more broadly, to many types of service for Christian communities.[44] But Jackson also suggests that as Martha was walking around the house setting up the meal for the disciples, she might have paused once or twice to listen to a teaching from Jesus that particularly spoke to her heart. She may have also been listening from the kitchen.

Medieval theologians read Luke 10:38-42 as an allegory for the relationship between the active and the contemplative lives. Theologians such as Meister Eckhart saw Mary and Martha as two sides of the same coin of the spiritual life: "today as feminists critique binary oppositions and dualistic either/or thinking, we must think instead of the importance of both sisters and their choices."[45] This illumination signifies the importance of Mary and Martha's contemplation in its use of the mandala imagery from *Genealogy of Jesus.*

41. Reid, *Wisdom's Feast,* 112–13.

42. Ibid., 105; Loveday C. Alexander, "Sisters in Adversity: Retelling Martha's Story," in *A Feminist Companion to Luke,* ed. Amy-Jill Levine and Marianne Blickenstaff (Cleveland, OH: Pilgrim Press, 2001), 197–213.

43. Susan Felch, "Reading and Re-Reading the Story of Martha and Mary" (paper presented at Midwest Conference on Christianity and Literature, Spring Arbor University, Spring Arbor, MI, February 19–20, 2016).

44. Reid, *Wisdom's Feast,* 107.

45. Ibid., 117–18.

Donald Jackson tells us that this imagery refers to "the birth of intellect," the human activity of making sense of the world around us.[46] Both sisters must contemplate the riddling parables in this illumination, must make sense of them in their own lives. Given that this pattern also appears in *Garden of Eden*, we are also invited to draw a connection between Eve as she gains knowledge of good and evil—a necessary step in the maturity of humankind—and Mary and Martha as they learn about forgiveness and the kingdom of heaven from Jesus. Mary and Martha's turned backs invite the viewer to join them *both* in Jesus' audience. Men and women alike can identify with the Mary-Martha dynamic. We are all Mary or Martha at different points in our lives.

One of the parables Mary and Martha contemplate contains a female image of God: the parable of the Lost Coin (Luke 15:8-10) in which the woman has nine coins and seeks one. The lost coin is the most important, the one worth rejoicing over once it is found. In this parable, God seeks the lost coin—the sinner lost to God. Jesus could have told this parable with a man searching for a coin, but instead he chooses a woman. The silver color of the coin connects the woman of the parable with Woman Wisdom. We may see this parable as a parable for today's Christian women searching for their stories in Scripture and in Christian history.[47] Even if those stories are little preserved, when they are found there is great rejoicing. Mary and Martha become the modern women of faith, struggling to balance contemplation and action in their own lives, claiming their narratives in the Bible and the Christian tradition.

WOMEN IN THE DEATH AND RESURRECTION OF JESUS

> Luke 23:44-49: *Crucifixion*
> John 20:1-31: *Resurrection*
> John 1:35-51: *Call of the Disciples*
> Luke 7:36-50: *Dinner at the Pharisee's House*

The gospels' narratives of the presence of women at the foot of the cross and the empty tomb provide sources for women's spirituality and witness today. Though the identities of the women at the cross vary among the four evangelists, each gospel features *women* as those who first find the empty

---

46. Calderhead, *Illuminating the Word*, 191.

47. Linda Maloney, "'Swept Under the Rug': Feminist Hermeneutical Reflections on the Parable of the Lost Coin (Lk. 15.8–9)," in *The Lost Coin: Parables of Women, Work, and Wisdom*, ed. Mary Ann Beavis, The Biblical Seminar 86 (London: Sheffield Academic Press, 2002), 35–37.

tomb, giving the gospel writer a chance to demonstrate the faith of the female disciples apart from the male twelve. Through its repeated imagery, *The Saint John's Bible* heightens the role of these women. The illuminations especially focus on Mary Magdalene, the only woman present at both the cross and the empty tomb in all four gospels.

The only illumination of the passion narrative in *The Saint John's Bible* is *Crucifixion* in Luke, which features a subtle allusion to the presence of the women at the foot of the cross. A purely golden Christ shines on the cross, which is askew like the world is topsy-turvy when Jesus dies. The

Donald Jackson, Luke 23:44-49: *Crucifixion*

crooked cross contrasts with the upright pillar of light in *Birth of Jesus*.[48] An often overlooked feature of this illumination is the subtle gold lace pattern around its borders. This lace appears in only one other book: the Song of Solomon, which features a woman yearning for her male beloved, often allegorized as God or Jesus. The lace border in *I Am My Beloved's* (Song 6:3) evokes the presence of the women at the foot of the cross in all four gospels, especially Mary Magdalene and Mary, mother of Jesus. In making this connection, *The Saint John's Bible* repeats an association in medieval Western liturgy between the woman in the Song and the lament of Jesus' mother, who likewise cries out for her beloved at the foot of the cross. This lament is captured in the art of the *pietà* and the music of the *Stabat Mater*.[49]

The lace also suggests a close intimacy between Jesus and Mary Magdalene. Like Mary, mother of Jesus, Mary Magdalene is a key figure for feminist interpreters. While defending Mary Magdalene against the medieval charge that she was a prostitute, these exegetes sing Mary's positive praises as well: she is the "first disciple of the Risen Jesus,"[50] and "the only known disciple whose faithfulness to Jesus does not waver."[51] *The Saint John's Bible* gives her a full-page treatment in *Resurrection*, which depicts the key moment in John 20 when Jesus tells her not to hold on to him, for he has not yet ascended.

In this image, she has already recognized him, as she calls out "*Rabbouni!*" in the Aramaic letters next to her. The focus is on Mary Magdalene's face lit by Jesus, rather than on the enigmatic back of Christ himself. Like Mary Magdalene, we too must let go of Jesus' physical form, as we cannot see his face in this illumination. Jesus' light on Mary Magdalene alludes to the theme of the duality of light and darkness running throughout John's gospel. Jesus is the light. The look on her face is enlightened wonder.

The Saint John's Bible subtly hints at Mary Magdalene in two other Gospels illuminations. A swatch of her dress appears in *Call of the Disciples*, a text that omits the female disciples. Jackson implies that Mary Magdalene is

48. Fanucci, "Variation on a Theme," 28.

49. William Flynn, "*In Persona Mariae*: Singing the Song of Songs as a Passion Commentary," in *Perspectives on the Passion: Encountering the Bible through the Arts*, ed. Christine Joynes and Nancy Macky (London: Bloomsbury T&T Clark, 2008), 106–21.

50. Gail R. O'Day, "Gospel of John," in *Women's Bible Commentary*, ed. Carol A. Newsom, Sharon H. Ringe, and Jacqueline E. Lapsley, 3rd ed. (Louisville, KY: Westminster John Knox, 2012), 529.

51. Kyndall Renfro, "Faithful Disciple, Feminine Witness: Mary Magdalene Revisited," *Review & Expositor* 110, no. 1 (2013): 131.

Donald Jackson, John 20:1-31: *Resurrection*

Donald Jackson, John 1:35-51:
Call of the Disciples

a disciple on a par with the men, even though no gospel narrates the story of her call. This fragment of her dress is in the edge of the illumination, signifying the marginalization of women as disciples of Jesus. Yet in John 20, she is front and center, while the men are absent.

Likewise, Mary Magdalene's dark skin, awe-filled expression, and red dress in *Resurrection* strongly resemble that of the woman with the alabaster

" For John the Baptist has come eating no bread & drinking no wine, and you say, 'He has a demon; the Son of Man has come eating & drinking, and you say, 'Look, a glutton and a drunkard, a friend of tax collectors and sinners!' Nevertheless, wisdom is vindicated by all her children." One of the Pharisees asked Jesus to eat with him, and he went into the Pharisee's house and took his place at the table. And a woman in the city, who was a sinner, having learned that he was eating in the Pharisee's house, brought an alabaster jar of ointment. She

to the woman, Your faith has saved you; go in peace.

HER SINS WHICH WERE MANY, HAVE BEEN FORGIVEN; HENCE SHE HAS SHOWN GREAT LOVE.

YOU GAVE ME NO KISS

Donald Jackson, Luke 7:36-50: *Dinner at the Pharisee's House*

jar in *Dinner at the Pharisee's House.* This woman is frequently conflated with Mary Magdalene in Christian tradition, though the text does not make that identification.[52] Her expression is one of humble determination—a sinner striving to serve Jesus despite the ridicule she receives from others in the house. Jackson focuses on this face, leaving Simon the Pharisee out of the illumination. The woman with the alabaster jar and Mary Magdalene have a similar face. Their dark skin is uncharacteristic of Western Christian art, which often depicts the Judeans of the New Testament as pale-skinned Europeans. By connecting these women, *The Saint John's Bible* evokes the interconnected network of illuminations highlighting the role of female disciples in Jesus' life and ministry. Jackson's paintings of Mary Magdalene ask us: "Do you see this woman?"[53]

52. Brittany E. Wilson, "Mary Magdalene and Her Interpreters," in *Women's Bible Commentary*, ed. Carol A. Newsom, Sharon H. Ringe, and Jacqueline E. Lapsley, 3rd ed. (Louisville, KY: Westminster John Knox, 2012), 532.

53. Barbara E. Reid, *Choosing the Better Part? Women in the Gospel of Luke* (Collegeville, MN: Michael Glazier, 1996), 122.

THE WOMAN AND THE DRAGON: THE SUM OF ALL BIBLICAL WOMEN

Revelation 12:1-18: *Woman and the Dragon*

Most of the books of *The Saint John's Bible* are a collaboration between multiple scribes and illuminators. But for the grand finale of the project, Jackson decided he would write and illuminate the book of Revelation entirely on his own. As he did so, he drew on the repertoire of symbols and motifs he had created for the previous seven volumes, making Revelation's illuminations echo themes throughout the Bible. The illumination of the *Woman and the Dragon* in Revelation 12 symbolically unifies many of the powerful models of womanhood throughout *The Saint John's Bible*, from Eve to Mary Magdalene.

Modern readers of Revelation 12 have pointed out that this passage provides an empowering image of feminine courage. The woman is described in royal, astrological terms. Her power over the moon and the stars indicates that she controls the fate of the universe. Her crown signifies her royalty. The woman is often interpreted as Mary, mother of Jesus, or as a symbol of the persecuted church. But while the woman is a prominent *image*, the actual *agents* in this story are men. The woman is both under attack by a male serpent and defended by a male archangel, Michael.[54] In Jackson's illumination, however, Michael is represented only by his sword. The art focuses on the woman.

Her body language is clear: confronting a serpent trying to devour her soon-to-be-born baby, she places her hand firmly on her belly, showing her maternal protectiveness. Jackson used his wife,

Donald Jackson, Revelation 12:1-18: *Woman and the Dragon*

---

54. Dorothy A. Lee, "The Heavenly Woman and the Dragon: Rereadings of Revelation 12," in *Feminist Poetics of the Sacred: Creative Suspicions*, ed. Frances Devlin-Glass and Lyn McCredden, American Academy of Religion Cultural Criticism Series (Oxford: Oxford University Press, 2001), 203–4.

Mabel Jackson, as the model for this hand.[55] While the text does not tell us about her emotions and experiences, Jackson paints on her face a powerful, determined gaze, not fear or desperation.

This woman, however, does not stand alone. *The Saint John's Bible* sets her in solidarity with many other women in the Bible. The serpent attacking her is the coral snake that tempts Eve. Her headdress is that of Esther. Her garment is both Mary Magdalene's *and* Jesus' cloaks in *Resurrection*, and is supplemented by a royal purple streak. Her face is that of Mary Magdalene and the woman with the alabaster jar—the dark skin of an indigenous woman.[56] Through this image's summing-up of many other biblical women, Jackson creates an image for Christian women today: not fearful, but determined, drawing on biblical witnesses such as Eve, Mary Magdalene, Esther, and Woman Wisdom herself.

WOMAN WISDOM

> Wisdom of Solomon 7:22b-30: *Wisdom Woman*
> Sirach 24:1-34: *Praise of Wisdom*
> Sirach 35: *She Is a Reflection*
> Proverbs 31:10-31: *Woman of Valor*
> Sirach 6:14-22: *Faithful Friends*
> Wisdom of Solomon 7: Correction bee
> Sirach 39:13-15: *Listen*
> Sirach 51: Carpet page

For the Wisdom Books, Jackson and the Committee chose to focus on Woman Wisdom, the most prominent feminine image of God in the Old Testament, also known as Sophia.[57] Throughout the Wisdom tradition of ancient Israel, wisdom was frequently personified as a woman. Woman Wisdom is described as both an aspect and a creation of God, dwelling in

---

55. Calderhead, *Illuminating the Word*, 260.

56. Jonathan Juilfs, "Medieval Apocalypse Books and *The St John's Bible* Book of Revelation" (paper presented at Midwest Conference on Christianity and Literature, Spring Arbor University, Spring Arbor, MI, February 19–20, 2016).

57. "Woman Wisdom" is translated from the Hebrew term ḥākmâ, "wisdom," rendered in Greek as *sophia*. Feminist scholars sometimes prefer Sophia because the word "suggests a person rather than a concept." Here we use Woman Wisdom to emphasize the Hebrew, Old Testament context of these illuminations rather than the Greek. Susan Cole, Marian Ronan, and Hal Taussig, *Wisdom's Feast: Sophia in Study and Celebration*, new ed. (Kansas City, MO: Sheed & Ward, 1996), 16.

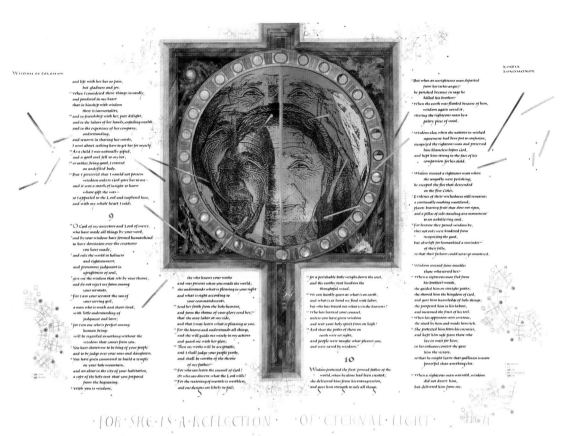

Donald Jackson, Wisdom of Solomon 7:22b-30: *Wisdom Woman*

Israel and working in its history, promising prosperity and blessing to those who follow her.[58] Some feminist scholars even argue that she is the remnant of a goddess tradition in Israel. Woman Wisdom is the bridge between the human and the divine, and is an architect of creation.[59]

While gold represents the presence of God throughout *The Saint John's Bible*, silver or platinum represents the presence of Woman Wisdom.[60] The premier image of Woman Wisdom in *The Saint John's Bible* is *Wisdom*

58. Roland E. Murphy, *The Tree of Life: An Exploration of Biblical Wisdom Literature* (Grand Rapids, MI: Eerdmans, 2002), 133–49.

59. Irene Nowell, *Women in the Old Testament* (Collegeville, MN: Liturgical Press, 1997), 139; Murphy, *The Tree of Life*, 145.

60. Sink, *The Art of* The Saint John's Bible, 98.

Woman, which accompanies a long homage to Wisdom in Wisdom of Solomon. This illumination depicts Woman Wisdom as an old woman, beaming at the viewer in a silver mirror with a smile described as "knowing" and "secretive," but also intimate.[61] The image is a silkscreen of a photo of an elderly Palestinian woman that Donald Jackson had in his studio for several decades. He did not know why he was attracted to this photo, but when he was brainstorming this illumination, he realized it would fit perfectly.[62] Her smile and age convey that she is wise and experienced, willing to share her wisdom with those who accept her invitation. Just as Woman Wisdom is playful and joyful (Prov 8:30), so is *Wisdom Woman*.

The mirror-shaped illumination echoes Wisdom 7:26, which describes Woman Wisdom as "a reflection of eternal light, a spotless mirror of the working of God, and an image of his goodness." Just as *Jesus with Mary and Martha* invites viewers to join Mary and Martha listening to Jesus, so this illumination reflects to its viewer the question: How might *you* reflect Wisdom? The Arab calendric diagram around her face in the mirror shows the twenty-eight phases of the moon.[63] The moon is traditionally a feminine symbol, associated with the menstrual cycle. The silver and gold bars around the central portrait allude to the presence of God and Woman Wisdom—the mutuality of masculine and feminine images of God.[64]

In the New Testament, the Old Testament's image of Woman Wisdom as companion of God becomes Jesus, the Son of God. *The Saint John's Bible* makes this connection through the astronomical imagery in the four corners of the mirror in *Wisdom Woman* and in *Word Made Flesh*, the frontispiece to John's gospel. This imagery meditates on both Woman Wisdom and the Cosmic Christ at creation. The figure of Christ in *Word Made Flesh* is half formed, as if the viewer sees the incarnation *in media res*—perhaps even without a definite gender yet.

The exaltation of Woman Wisdom continues in Suzanne Moore's *Praise of Wisdom*. Moore invites us to join Woman Wisdom in exalting the beauty of God's handiwork. Though this illumination shows Moore's highly abstract style, symbols in the piece reflect the agricultural imagery in the text. The leaves and fruit reflect floral metaphors for Wisdom (Sir 24:13-17). The

---

61. Ibid., 132.

62. Christopher Calderhead, "Computer Meets Quill: The Making of a Contemporary Manuscript Bible," *Anglican Theological Review* 83, no. 4 (September 2001): 235.

63. Patella, *Word and Image*, 176.

64. On this point I am indebted to Anne Kaese.

warm brown colors of the illumination allude to Wisdom's being sweeter than honey (Sir 24:20), and the patch of the blue on the right side of the image links it to water imagery (Sir 24:25-31). The pattern at top right looks like a cross, but also reflects prehistoric fertility statues, which, according to some, represent cultic statues from goddess worship of prehistoric Europe.[65] The lines in the lower left draw from the supposed sacred script associated with these goddess figurines.[66] Indeed, according to current Old Testament scholars, the biblical Woman Wisdom may be a remnant of worship of the goddess Asherah in ancient Israel. At bottom right a subtle cross image alludes to Jesus' agricultural abundance in *Loaves and Fishes* in Mark. Women are the life-bearers in the human realm: Moore's agricultural plenty alludes back to her *Ruth the Gleaner* with its basket of wheat. As Moore says, the oldest feminine symbol is "the abundance of the table."[67] Woman Wisdom dances across the pages in silver half circles—according to Moore, half-moons. The beauty of creation hints at the presence of God in the female Wisdom.

Suzanne Moore, Sirach 24:1-34:
Praise of Wisdom

All five scribes who worked on Wisdom Books added their own homage to Woman Wisdom in the form of five marginal text treatments.[68] Many of these treatments are not located next to the text of that verse, but are placed throughout the volume. Two of these focus on texts not otherwise treated: Wisdom 6:12, located at Job 15, and Sirach 1:16. The other three feature texts also treated in illuminations: Sirach 24:19, found at Sirach 13; Sirach 24:12, 13, 15-17, found at Sirach 44; and Wisdom 7:26, found at Sirach 35.

---

65. According to Suzanne Moore, the images she drew on can be found in Marija Gimbutas, *The Civilization of the Goddess: The World of Old Europe*, ed. Joan Marler (New York: HarperCollins, 1991), 75, 84, 170, 246, 311.

66. Marija Gimbutas, *The Living Goddesses*, ed. Miriam Robbins Dexter (Berkeley: University of California Press, 2001), chap. 2, "Symbols, Signs, and Sacred Script"; Cari Ferraro, "Goddess in the Bible," *Alphabet* 34, no. 3 (Summer 2009): 20–25.

67. Much of the information in this paragraph comes from Suzanne Moore, personal communication, July 7, 2017.

68. Sink, *The Art of* The Saint John's Bible, 105.

Susie Lieper, Sirach 35:
She Is a Reflection

This last text treatment includes the yin-yang symbol from Daoist philosophy and art. We might see this as a symbol of the relationship between masculine and feminine images of God: both necessary, neither by itself sufficient in grasping the mystery of a God who is beyond gender. The silver background again points to Woman Wisdom.

Wisdom is not only an abstract personification of a divine figure. She is present in the workings of ordinary human women. Proverbs 31, *Woman of Valor*, is often read by feminist interpreters as a hymn to Wisdom.[69] Hazel Dolby meditates on this passage using the image of a colorful tapestry—the symbol par excellence of women in *The Saint John's Bible*, here in a rich royal purple.

Weaving and textile making are mentioned throughout Proverbs 31 as activities of the woman of valor, for whom "strength and dignity are her clothing" (Prov 31:25). To create this image, Hazel Dolby "looked at the role of African women in family life: the nurturing of children, plants, animals, the home and cooking [and] also the role of women in the community: valued for their wisdom and practicality."[70] Indeed, one wonders if the figure of Woman Wisdom is born not from goddess worship, but from the archetypal role of grandmothers in conveying cultural knowledge and stories. Proverbs 31 does not just idealize women's work, but "theologically legitimate[s]" the labor of women as a means of instruction and an example of godliness.[71] As three modern feminist writers ask,

> What happens to women when they become aware of Sophia's divine power within themselves? . . . Women begin to value their own thoughts, feelings, and experiences. Through Sophia's presence in their lives what they think becomes important, what they feel becomes legitimate, what they experience becomes real.[72]

69. Christine Roy Yoder, "Proverbs," in *Women's Bible Commentary*, ed. Carol A. Newsom, Sharon H. Ringe, and Jacqueline E. Lapsley, 3rd ed. (Louisville, KY: Westminster John Knox, 2012), 241.

70. Calderhead, *Illuminating the Word*, 229.

71. Yoder, "Proverbs," 242.

72. Cole, Ronan, and Taussig, *Wisdom's Feast*, 63.

Woman Wisdom does not pray in eternal seclusion in a contemplative realm. Wisdom reveals Her message in everyday life and through ordinary people, especially women.

The woman of Proverbs 31 is not only Woman Wisdom but may also be any of the human biblical women examined in this chapter. Hazel Dolby's illumination includes the image of a bee. The Hebrew word for "bee," *devorah*, connects this image to Deborah and *Deborah Anthology*. The hymn to the woman of valor in Proverbs 31 could be Deborah or any other woman—including any female reader of this Bible. The honeybee as image of Woman Wisdom appears again in the text treatments to Sirach 6:14-22 and 39:13-15, passages extolling Woman Wisdom. Diane Von Arx's treatments of these passages include honeycomb patterns in the background, drawn from the church of Saint John's Abbey for her treatment of 6:14-22, she includes a quilt pattern background continuing the theme of textiles and women.[73] Further,

Hazel Dolby, Proverbs 31:10-31:
Woman of Valor

Hazel Dolby, Proverbs 31:10-31:
Woman of Valor, detail

73. Diane Von Arx, personal communication, October 5, 2017.

Diane Von Arx, Sirach 6:14-22:
Faithful Friends

Sarah Harris and Chris Tomlin, Wisdom of Solomon 7:
Correction bee

the correction in Wisdom of Solomon 7 is a small bee hoisting the missing line into its proper place with a pulley system based on da Vinci's notebooks.[74]

In traditional Christian symbolism, the bee represents "activity, diligence, work, and order" as well as "sweetness and religious eloquence."[75] When

74. Sink, *The Art of* The Saint John's Bible, 133.

75. Ferguson, *Signs and Symbols in Christian Art*, 12.

Diane Von Arx, Sirach 39:13-15: *Listen*

Ezekiel eats the scroll initiating him as a prophet, he tells us that it "was as sweet as honey" (Ezek 3:3). Here, the sweet, diligent Woman Wisdom is Deborah and any other woman. Perhaps she is the diligent Martha, working hard to make possible the breaking of bread. Woman Wisdom places Scripture into its proper order. Without Wisdom's order, Scripture's words themselves would be out of place.

The last text treatment of Wisdom Books, Sirach 51's carpet page, echoes the floral imagery of Sirach 24:13-17. The Tree of Life comes right after a poem praising Wisdom in Sirach 51:13-30. Here the interconnected circles motif, found throughout *Wisdom Books*, forms a Tree of Life, another prominent symbol of wisdom in the Bible. The pattern is derived from an Indian textile with mirrors sewn in.[76] These circles in turn call to mind the moon cycle in *Wisdom Woman* and the pearls of knowledge that Wisdom gives forth. Underneath the tree is another verse praising Wisdom:

> She is a tree of life to those who lay hold of her;
> those who hold her fast are called happy. (Prov 3:18)

The colors of this tree echo the luscious reds and browns of the Song of Solomon illuminations, *Garden of Desire* (Song 4:1-15) and *I Am My Beloved's* (Song 6:3), further conveying the femininity and intimacy of Wisdom.[77] This circular motif also appears in *Woman and the Dragon*. Woman Wisdom *is* the Tree of Life (Sir 24:12-19).

76. Sink, *The Art of* The Saint John's Bible, 102.
77. Ibid., 143.

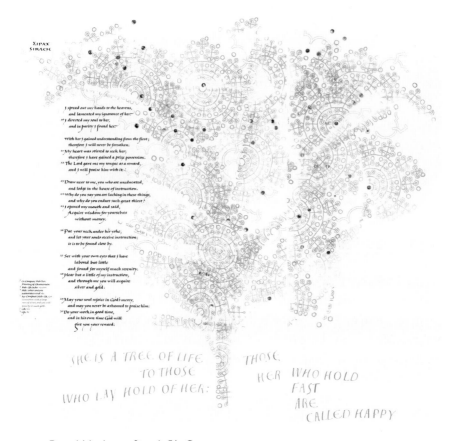

Donald Jackson, Sirach 51: Carpet page

CONCLUSION

In sum, the symbolism of textiles and silver and the foregrounding of women in *The Saint John's Bible* invite the reader to consider women's witness to godliness and justice in our own time. Beginning this chapter with the Tree of Knowledge of Good and Evil, we concluded it with the Tree of Life. Woman Wisdom, as the Tree of Life, reverses the rupture of our intimacy with God created by the rebellious eating of the fruit of the Tree of Knowledge. In the sacramental imagination, in which God is radically present in creation, *many* Trees of Life give us intimacy with God: the trees in our own backyard.

Chapter Four

EVERY LIVING TREE
Caring for Creation

Our very contact with nature has a deep restorative power; contemplation of its magnificence imparts peace and serenity. The Bible speaks again and again of the goodness and beauty of creation, which is called to glorify God.

—Pope John Paul II

P ope John Paul II spoke these words in his visionary homily for the 1990 World Day of Peace, ushering in a Catholic movement for creation care and environmental justice. Popes John Paul II, Benedict XVI, and Francis have all stressed the importance of care for creation, culminating in Francis's recent encyclical *Laudato Si'*. The Catholic creation care movement is not merely a rebranded secular environmentalism, but a call rooted in "the Christian vision of a sacramental universe—a world that discloses the Creator's presence by visible and tangible signs."[1]

Glynis Mary McManamon, RGS, a nun and artist in Ferguson, MO, captures the Catholic vision of the sacramental universe in her painting *Protectress of the Poor*. She depicts the Earth in the cloaked embrace of a brown-skinned woman with a rainbow halo.[2] The woman's blue coat suggests

1. United States Conference of Catholic Bishops, *Renewing the Earth: An Invitation to Reflection and Action on Environment in Light of Catholic Social Teaching* (November 14, 1991), III.A.

2. Dawn Araujo-Hawkins, "Q & A with Sr. Glynis Mary McManamon, Moving People through Art," *Global Sisters Report*, June 23, 2016, http://globalsistersreport.org/blog/q /ministry/q-sr-glynis-mary-mcmanamon-moving-people-through-art-40536.

Sr. Glynis Mary McManamon, *Protectress of the Poor* (2016)

she is Mary, here as both the Black Madonna and Our Lady of Guadalupe, an image of Mary close to the hearts of the indigenous people here holding up the earth. McManamon suggests that just as Mary embraces the poor—the colonized indigenous people of earth—so she protects all creation. McManamon's image suggests the intimate connection in Catholic teaching between caring for Earth and caring for the indigenous people most affected by Earth's destruction.[3] The rainbow suggests hope. Perhaps the woman in this image is Wisdom.

3. Francis, *Laudato Si'*, On Care for Our Common Home (Vatican City: Libreria Editrice Vaticana, May 24, 2015), chap. 4.II.146.

Like John Paul II, Francis, and McManamon, *The Saint John's Bible* magnifies the significance of creation and calls its viewers to care for that creation. Through the repeated visual motifs of rainbows, wind, and other elements of nature, this Bible invites us to reflect on science as a way to better understand the beauty and complexity of creation, God's saving work through creation, Christ's renewal of the cosmos, and Woman Wisdom as the "Earth Mother" who is "spinning and weaving and webbing together Earth."[4] By combining imagery of Woman Wisdom and creation, Donald Jackson's art invites us to revere Mother Earth through all her trees of life, expanding our sacramental imagination to see nature's sustenance of humankind as a channel of God's grace. As Pope Francis writes, "Soil, water, mountains: everything is, as it were, a caress of God" (LS 84).

IN THE BEGINNING: CREATION IN GENESIS

Genesis 1:1–2:3: *Creation*
Genesis 2:4-25: *Garden of Eden*
Genesis 3:1-24: *Adam and Eve*

The illuminations of the seven days of creation, the Garden of Eden, and Adam and Eve set the scene for *The Saint John's Bible*'s subsequent treatment of creation. God's repeated refrain that his creation is *good* makes Genesis 1 a crucial text for contemporary Catholic creation care (see, for example, LS 65–67). These illuminations also remind us of the importance of science as a vehicle to understand creation.

The Saint John's Bible first emphasizes God as Creator of the *whole* cosmos in its choice to illuminate not the human-centric creation story in Genesis 2:4b-25, but the cosmic story in 1:1–2:4a. This image divides Genesis 1:1–2:4a's account of the seven days of creation into seven columns. One scholar calls this a "'geophany,' a manifestation or revelation of earth."[5]

---

4. Shirley Wurst, "Woman Wisdom's Way: Ecokinship," in *The Earth Story in Wisdom Traditions*, ed. Norman C. Habel and Shirley Wurst, The Earth Bible 3 (Sheffield: Sheffield Academic Press, 2001), 54.

5. Norman C. Habel, "Geophany: The Earth Story in Genesis 1," in *The Earth Story in Genesis*, ed. Norman C. Habel and Shirley Wurst, The Earth Bible 2 (Sheffield: Sheffield Academic, 2000), 35.

Donald Jackson, Genesis 1:1–2:3: *Creation*

The ecological message of Genesis 1–2 is that while humans are important, while we have dominion over creation and the power to name the other creatures, we are only the final touch to a universe that God deemed good *before* we entered it. We are a *part* of creation, not above it or separate from it. Like every other animal, we are dependent on Mother Earth for survival.

In this way, Genesis 1–2 coincides surprisingly well with modern science. Humans are distinctive—we have language, for example. But we evolved from other mammals and continue to share the greater proportion of our DNA with them. Jackson alludes to this new perspective on humankind's origins by including scientific imagery in *Creation*. The chaos and formlessness, the *tohu wabohu* in Hebrew, are illuminated as disjointed fractal patterns evoking the birth of a star. The fish in the sea are images of fossils and a school of fish alluding to the centrality of community for all life on Earth. Most importantly, the creation of humankind is depicted using prehistoric cave art from Australia and Africa. This cave art reminds us of the scientific account of humanity's origins in primates. Rather than any kind of "war" between science and religion, this illumination reflects the Catholic idea that scientific truth leads to God. As Jackson explains, "I find that the Genesis story fits a lot of science."[6] Science is not just a theory that can be *reconciled with* Scripture, but another *window into* the glory of God's creation.

One aspect that often puzzles viewers of *Creation* is the raven in the center. Would it not make more sense to include the dove from the Flood? Noah, however, sent a raven to find land before he sent the dove. One legend about St. Benedict recalls him feeding ravens in the wilderness, one of many references in *The Saint John's Bible* to its Benedictine patron. Also, ravens fed Elijah in the Wadi Cherith (1 Kgs 17:4-6). Black birds such as ravens commonly congregate at the Saint John's University campus and at Jackson's Scriptorium.[7] Perhaps this is not a black raven but the shadow of the white dove who is the Holy Spirit, present whenever "two or three are gathered" (Matt 18:20) reading *The Saint John's Bible*.[8] Jackson comments, "Ravens are dark, powerful, they have that strong wingbeat. . . . The raven represents power, continually flying, tireless, endless. It's taking us for a ride across space and time," a kind of cosmic traveler.[9] Maybe the raven is God.

Garden of Eden and *Adam and Eve* continue a close look at creation through careful observation, incorporating more prehistoric cave art and fish fossil imagery. *Adam and Eve* depicts the first two humans as of African

---

6. Calderhead, *Illuminating the Word*, 190.

7. Ibid.

8. Jason Paul Engel, personal communication, June 2017.

9. Calderhead, *Illuminating the Word*, 190.

descent, based on images of the Karo people of southwest Ethiopia, in keeping with the scientific theory that humankind came out of Africa.[10] *Garden of Eden* also includes many images of deadly animals that look beautiful, just as the fruit on the Tree of the Knowledge of Good and Evil was tempting to the senses but painful for the soul. These images, drawn and painted by natural history illustrator Chris Tomlin, reflect a close attention to nature's details.

Already the very first three pages of *The Saint John's Bible* reveal a rich conversation about creation in relation to order, science, and human nature. Jackson includes intertextual connections through verses written in the right and left margins around Genesis 2–3. Previously we discussed the quote from 2 Corinthians 3:18 evoking *Wisdom Woman*. On the left, a quote from Romans 8:19 points forward to a significant creation-related illumination in Romans. These three illuminations set the tone for the theme of creation throughout the rest of this Bible.

CREATION: FROM CHAOS TO ORDER

Ecclesiastes 1:1-11: *Ecclesiastes Frontispiece*
Mark 16: *Milkweed and Butterfly*
Proverbs 8:22–9:6: *Pillars of Wisdom*

The creation story in Genesis 1:1–2:4a depicts the construction of the cosmos as an orderly affair. The writers of biblical Wisdom literature looked to creation to understand human life: "Reflection on life and observation of nature led the sages to conclude that there is a kind of order inherent in creation. They believed that if they could discern how this order operated and harmonize their lives in accord with it, they would live peacefully and fruitfully."[11] The sages' profound poems about creation lend themselves well to an ecological engagement with Scripture.

The sage who wrote Ecclesiastes had a famously tough time discerning the "order inherent in creation." Rather than the architecture of Genesis 1:1–2:4a, *Ecclesiastes Frontispiece* depicts chaos creeping into that order, reflecting this sage's difficulty finding meaning in the mess of life. Jackson's illumination spills out over two pages in an asymmetrical, borderless bedlam.

10. Sink, *The Art of* The Saint John's Bible, 10.
11. Dianne Bergant, *A New Heaven, A New Earth: The Bible and Catholicity* (Maryknoll, NY: Orbis Books, 2016), 89.

This tornado, evoked by gray swirling lines, reflects a verse at the beginning of the book:

> The wind blows to the south,
>   and goes around to the north;
> round and round goes the wind,
>   and on its circuits the wind returns. (Eccl 1:6)

The futile circuit of the wind becomes a metaphor for the futile exertions of our own lives. The word for "vanity" in Ecclesiastes's famous line "all is vanity!" (Eccl 1:2) can also be translated as "breath" or "wind." Here the whirlwinds reach even beyond the borders of the physical page.

The whirlwind sweeps up different creatures of the sky. The raven at the center immediately connects this illumination to *Creation*. If the raven is an allusion to the Flood, then this illumination reflects the chaos of the heavy

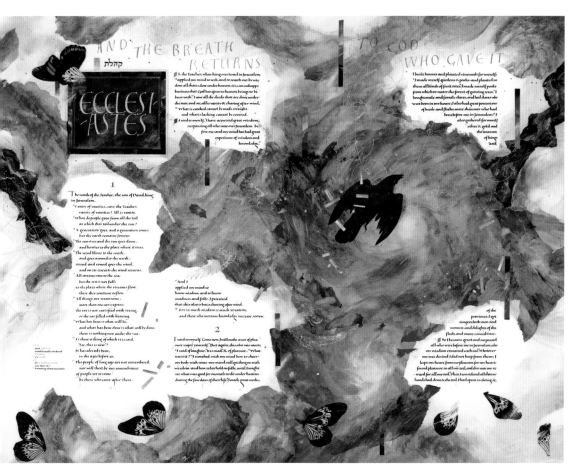

Donald Jackson, Ecclesiastes 1:1-11: *Ecclesiastes Frontispiece*

winds that Noah sheltered from in his ship. The butterfly wings, a common motif in *The Saint John's Bible*, are blown about seemingly unattached to any butterflies, a symbol, as Jackson says, of "flimsiness."[12] Jackson comments that butterflies are an "analogy for angels . . . beautiful, full of grace, fragile and very mysterious in a funny kind of way."[13] Their chaos contrasts with the orderly life cycle of the butterfly as depicted in Chris Tomlin's illumination at the end of Mark's gospel. Here the butterfly is an allegory for Christ. Just as the caterpillar appears to die in its chrysalis "tomb," so Christ seemed to be dead forever but came back from the grave.

Chris Tomlin, Mark 16:
Milkweed and Butterfly

Still, Jackson insinuates ordered creation. Seven small columns of rainbow patterns refer to God's promise to Noah after the Flood. Although there is no illumination of the Flood in *The Saint John's Bible*, the rainbow appears throughout this Bible as a symbol of God's love in his covenant with Noah. Just as Noah was delivered from his suffering and received the assurance of God's promise, so perhaps the writer of Ecclesiastes will be too. In the upper right, Jackson inserts an astronomical diagram from a medieval Arab scientific treatise. As Jackson comments, "the bright colours represent life's joys while the moon's waxing and waning represent the ups and downs of our earthly life."[14] This is reminiscent of the cycle of the moon in *Creation* and *Wisdom Woman*, representing Wisdom's role as architect of creation.[15] The diagram of the moon cycle represents both order in creation and the human attempt to discern that order through scientific investigation and observation—perhaps guided by Woman Wisdom.

Despite the chaotic winds, the strong, steady raven stays its course even as the butterflies—the angels—are scattered by the winds. Jackson comments that the raven is a natural evocation of death, which the writer of Ecclesiastes keeps so large in his own mind.[16] Death certainly is

12. Calderhead, *Illuminating the Word*, 231.
13. Ibid., 197.
14. Ibid., 230.
15. Ibid.
16. Ibid.

a certainty in life. But perhaps the raven is God himself, or Woman Wisdom herself, maintaining order in the midst of chaos.

The circularity of life discerned by the sage in Ecclesiastes has another ecological dimension. Much of humanity's destruction of the environment stems from our relentless quest for more: clearing forests to build sky-scrapers, "pav[ing] paradise to put up a parking lot."[17] Yet in Ecclesiastes's vision, "human striving for gain is nothing but wearisome labor that must be repeated and repeated with no promise of completion and no assurance of gratification."[18] Buildings will be bulldozed, and concrete will crumble and crack. If we take a long-term view in line with Francis's vision of integral ecology, we might question the need for newer, bigger, more unsustainable building projects and their impacts on our air, water, soil, and all other manifestations of creation. With Ecclesiastes, we might decide to be content with less striving and more "eat[ing], and drink[ing], and enjoy[ing] [our] selves" (Eccl 8:15).

In *Ecclesiastes Frontispiece*, the chaos in the life of the sage is writ large in the cosmos; in *Pillars of Wisdom*, Woman Wisdom invites us to discern God's cosmic order in her house. This illumination replicates Ecclesiastes's whirlwind background. Beneath the stormy weather stands the house of Wisdom, where the winds have calmed into flat horizontal lines: order rather than chaos. The house itself is built with pillars, requiring planning and math, lending structure and stability. The seven pillars of this house (Eccl 9:1) allude to the number seven's biblical meaning of "rest, fulfillment, and restoration."[19] *Ecclesiastes Frontispiece* has seven rainbow bars. *The Saint John's Bible* has seven volumes. *Creation* portrays creation in seven days using seven columns.

In this house of Wisdom, the pillars are also the seven burning candles of the menorah, one flaming brightly with Woman Wisdom's interconnected circles motif associated with her Tree of Life. The silver circle of the candle flame could just as well be the moon in *Wisdom Woman*'s moon cycle, one of the lost coins in *Luke Anthology*, or one of Wisdom's pearls—like the pearl of great price in Jesus' parable (Matt 13:45-46). At the bottom of the page, Woman Wisdom invites the reader to "eat of my bread and drink of

---

17. Joni Mitchell, "Big Yellow Taxi," *Ladies of the Canyon* (Los Angeles: A&M Records, 1970).

18. Bergant, *A New Heaven, a New Earth*, 95.

19. Keith A. Burton, "Numbers," ed. David Noel Freedman, *Eerdmans Dictionary of the Bible* (Grand Rapids, MI: Eerdmans, 2000), 974.

Donald Jackson, Proverbs 8:22–9:6: *Pillars of Wisdom*

the wine I have mixed" (Prov 9:5), depicted here in eucharistic terms. The house of Wisdom is the temple with its lampstands, but also the church with its Eucharist, all three of which are ordered and structured by Wisdom.

If Ecclesiastes struggles to see the order in creation, *Pillars of Wisdom* reestablishes that structure. Benedict XVI preaches that "many people experience peace and tranquillity, renewal and reinvigoration, when they come into close contact with the beauty and harmony of nature."[20] The house of Wisdom, or the church, is the place where God as Creator—and hence God as beauty-maker and harmony-maker—is proclaimed. Ecclesiastes's turmoil resolves in Wisdom's house.

20. Benedict XVI, "If You Want to Cultivate Peace, Protect Creation" (homily, World Day of Peace, Vatican City, January 1, 2010), 13.

CREATION AND HUMAN DELIVERANCE

Wisdom of Solomon 13:1-5: *Creation, Covenant, Shekinah, Kingdom*
Job 1-2: *Job Frontispiece*
Job 38:1–42:6: *Out of the Whirlwind, Where Were You*
Job 42:7-17: *Out of the Whirlwind, He Will Wipe Every Tear*

God not only made the world, but God can use that world—the land, the sea, all living beings—to send messages to humankind and deliver us from affliction. The Bible tells many stories of God doing so, such as the parting of the Sea of Reeds enabling the Israelites to escape their Egyptian bondage. God does not only act in creation on a large scale for all of Israel; God also creates theophanies in nature on a smaller scale for individuals. *The Saint John's Bible* focuses on stories of both.

God's dramatic, large-scale actions in creation are captured in *Creation, Covenant, Shekinah, Kingdom* in Wisdom of Solomon. This passage calls its audience to worship the one God who created the elements of nature: "If through delight in the beauty of these things people assumed them to be gods, let them know how much better than these is their Lord, for the author of beauty created them" (Wis 13:3). This illumination's four panels, depicting earth, air, fire, and water—the elements of nature (Wis 13:2)—also focus on Wisdom's presence at various moments in the sacred history of Israel.

The first panel visually quotes *Creation* in Genesis: the creation of the moon and stars, the creatures of the earth, and humankind (Wis 9:2, 9:9, 10:10). The raven from *Creation* and *Ecclesiastes Frontispiece* makes another appearance. The second panel, air, alludes to the Flood, with the dove midair representing both Noah's dove and the Holy Spirit (Wis 10:4). The third panel, fire, is the burning bush, with Hebrew letters spelling the *Shekinah* (divine presence) of

Donald Jackson, Wisdom of Solomon 13:1-5: *Creation, Covenant, Shekinah, Kingdom*

God with the Israelites in the desert (Wis 10:17). The flames of the burning bush in turn allude to the "divided tongues, as of fire" (Acts 2:3) of the *Pentecost* illumination (Acts 2:1-39), paralleling the way in which theophany through flame guides both Israel and the church in their beginnings.

Finally, the fourth panel, water, alludes to the parting of the Sea of Reeds that enables the Israelites to escape Egypt (10:18). This panel also quotes from the illumination to Ezekiel's *Vision of the New Temple* (Ezek 40:1–48:35) "that focuses on the abundance provided to the people in the Promised Land and the eschatological meaning of the temple."[21] As in *Pillars of Wisdom*, the temple is the house of Wisdom, where God's order and design is most apparent. *Creation, Covenant, Shekinah, Kingdom* shows God behind each element of creation. Jackson's artistic designs that spill out beyond the margins are both a hallmark of his style and a hint that, to echo Michael Himes on the sacramental imagination, God's grace flows beyond our concepts and understanding.[22] In these panels, the gold and silver motifs point to the presence of both God and Wisdom, the balance of feminine and masculine images of the divine. Not only did God *create* the earth, air, fire, and water, but God also continues to reveal herself through these natural elements to reach out to humanity.

Even those who do not experience the wondrous theophanies that Noah and Moses did can find God in creation in more prosaic ways. Job finds himself tested when God takes away all his wealth, reputation, and children. Much of the book of Job is taken up with various approaches to the question of *how* God could allow such painful suffering. Yet Job's anguished question is not answered with a logical proof but by God himself, appearing in a whirlwind and interrogating Job (Job 38–42). *Where were you, Job, when I was creating the heavens and the earth? Can you, Job, fathom even a tenth of my divine understanding? No? Then do not question my doings*—says God.

God's speeches in Job 38–42 are simultaneously theophany and geophany. God speaks of a divine design beyond the narrow imaginings of any human, a design that broadens the individual's viewpoint out of his or her myopic misunderstanding. Even before God restores Job's wealth back to him, Job finds solace and much-needed perspective in contemplating the grand scheme of God's creation. These speeches are not just poetry; "the beauty of the divine speeches in Job is not an accidental literary feature or merely a pleasant harmonious aesthetic, but revelation itself. The beauty in the storm is fearsome, wild, free. . . . Job's experience of beauty does

21. Sink, *The Art of* The Saint John's Bible, 137.
22. Himes, "Finding God in All Things: A Sacramental Worldview and Its Effects."

Donald Jackson, Job 1–2: *Job Frontispiece*

not explain his suffering, but it transforms him."[23] *The Saint John's Bible* illuminates both Job's sufferings and God's response with themes drawn from *Creation, Covenant, Shekinah, Kingdom*, representing previous times when God manifested in creation in dramatic ways.

Job Frontispiece is divided into two halves, representing the tension between order and chaos in Job's life as in that of the narrator of Ecclesiastes.

23. Kathleen M. O'Connor, "Wild, Raging Creativity: Job in the Whirlwind," in *Earth, Wind, and Fire: Biblical and Theological Perspectives on Creation*, ed. Carol J. Dempsey and Mary Margaret Pazdan (Collegeville, MN: Michael Glazier, 2004), 54.

On the right-hand side is a dark whirlwind, representing Job's sense of meaning shattered by his pain. On the left-hand side, we see an allusion to the fourth panel of *Creation, Covenant, Shekinah, Kingdom*, representing the Israelites crossing the Sea of Reeds to escape from Egypt—God's order and restoration. Part of this allusion is the leaf pattern, which also appears in Song of Solomon's *Garden of Desire* (Song 4:1-15), suggesting that Job's intimacy with God was like that of the lovers in the Song. Yet in the typical ambiguous and playful style of *The Saint John's Bible*, the two halves of this illumination could just as easily be read in the opposite way. Perhaps the right-hand side is not a whirlwind of chaos, but the whirlwind from which God speaks and makes Job see his designs. Perhaps the left-hand side is not restoration, but Job's livestock and servants—his wealth—"already walking offstage."[24] We may also see the cattle and fish of this illumination as an allusion to Job's speech later in the book:

> But ask the animals, and they will teach you;
>   the birds of the air, and they will tell you;
> ask the plants of the earth, and they will teach you;
>   and the fish of the sea will declare to you.
> Who among all these does not know
>   that the hand of the Lord has done this?
> In his hand is the life of every living thing
>   and the breath of every human being. (Job 12:7-10)

Job challenges his friends to see that Wisdom is not only in Scripture. It rests even in animals and plants, for "it is precisely the integrity of creation following its inherent nature that these sages call human beings to emulate."[25] Not only do humans discern God's power and order, animals intuitively grasp it too.

Next to and above the animals and people is a bright red pattern of color reminiscent of the burning bush panel in *Creation, Covenant, Shekinah, Kingdom*. These allusions to the Exodus narrative connect Job's theophany of God speaking to him in the whirlwind with Moses' theophany at the burning bush and Israel's theophany in the parting of the Sea of Reeds. Job's deliverance at the end of his tale is like Israel's deliverance from Egypt into a land of milk and honey. Another symbol of Job's attempt to find order is the astronomical diagram in the upper-right corner. This diagram, also in

---

24. Sink, *The Art of* The Saint John's Bible, 101.
25. Bergant, *A New Heaven, a New Earth*, 96.

Creation and *Ecclesiastes Frontispiece*, alludes to the human desire to find order in the universe through scientific investigation—another kind of discerning of God's order in the world. Yet here the diagram is incomplete, cut off the page: Job, for most of the book, does not see God's cosmic design.

The frontispiece to Job alludes to God's speeches at the end of the book emphasizing the wonder of creation. In the words of nature writer Bill McKibben, "God is describing a world without people—a world that existed long before people . . . on a scale so powerful and vast that we are small indeed in the picture of things."[26] These speeches are themselves visualized by calligrapher Thomas Ingmire. The first text treatment highlights God's initial appearance "out of the whirlwind" (Job 38:1), and the Lord's interrogation pours out in a torrent of eleven questions. In the third part of the piece, the restoration of Job in 42:7-17 shoots upward, reflecting Job's new blessings from God.

Thomas Ingmire, Job 38:1–42:6: *Out of the Whirlwind, Where Were You*

26. Bill McKibben, *The Comforting Whirlwind: God, Job, and the Scale of Creation* (Cambridge, MA: Cowley Publications, 2005), 27.

Thomas Ingmire, *Job 42:7–17: Out of the Whirlwind, He Will Wipe Every Tear*

At the bottom of the third illumination, Ingmire adds a quote of Revelation 21:4 (which in turn quotes Isaiah 25:8) alluding to the new heaven and the new earth in John of Patmos's vision. This illumination bleeds through the vellum onto Ingmire's text treatment of Proverbs 1:7-8 on the next page, "suggesting that those who live by the wisdom taught in Proverbs need to be reminded that Job also lived by the same wisdom, and yet it did not guarantee him a happy, peaceful, successful pain-free life."[27] Though Job's life was suffused with pain and sorrow, he at least had the opportunity to see a larger divine order outside his personal scope.

In all three text treatments, God's words are underscored with the rainbow imagery found in *Ecclesiastes Frontispiece*. Just as *Job Frontispiece* depicts his suffering and deliverance in terms of the Exodus narrative, so *Out of the Whirlwind* juxtaposes Job with Noah. For Noah, Moses, and Israel, God makes his presence known through mighty wonders in creation. For Job, God makes his presence known in the wonder of the everyday working of creation rather than in any specific demonstration of divine power. In one perspective, "God speaks from the whirlwind . . . and we hear and see a creative and participant artist and artisan within an interconnected world whose vision embraces Earth's inhabitants from the least to the greatest."[28] For Noah, Moses, Israel, and Job, creation serves as a sacred site of God's human deliverance.

27. Jason Paul Engel, personal communication, June 2017.

28. Alice M. Sinnott, "Job 12: Cosmic Devastation and Social Turmoil," in *The Earth Story in Wisdom Traditions*, ed. Norman C. Habel and Shirley Wurst, The Earth Bible 3 (Sheffield: Sheffield Academic Press, 2001), 91.

WOMAN WISDOM AT CREATION

Wisdom of Solomon 7:22b-30: *Wisdom Woman*
Sirach 24:1-34: *Praise of Wisdom*

The sages of biblical Wisdom literature not only seek to teach wisdom but to evoke it as a personified figure in the form of Woman Wisdom. Illuminations pairing praise of Wisdom with her praise for creation invite us to join Wisdom in her own sense of wonder in God's creation. If Woman Wisdom was present at creation, a feminine image of God, then she is mother of Earth.

In *Wisdom Woman* (Wis 7:22b-30b), creation imagery in the borders of the mirror draws on the scientific imagery used also in *Creation* and *Genealogy of Jesus*. The author of Wisdom of Solomon proclaims that Woman Wisdom was present at the creation of the world (Wis 9:2, 9:9), and that she is even more beautiful than the sun and stars (Wis 7:29). The four corners of the mirror, each based on a Hubble telescope image, reflect the cosmic imagery in the text. Each corner represents elements of nature, alluding back to *Creation, Covenant, Shekinah, Kingdom*. The lower left corner represents fire, Moses' burning bush. The upper left evokes the expanse of the seemingly limitless universe, as on the first day *before* God created the earth. In contrast to the far reaches of outer space, encircling the mirror is a diagram of the twenty-eight stages of the more proximate lunar cycle, done in the silver of Woman Wisdom. The lunar cycle diagram serves as a counterpoint to the chaos in *Creation, Ecclesiastes Frontispiece*, and *Job Frontispiece*, and refers the viewer back to their astronomical diagrams.

The lunar cycle in *Wisdom Woman* interweaves woman, Wisdom, and creation: just as God ordained the cycle of the moon, so all women are tied to the moon through their menstrual cycle. Woman Wisdom reminds us that "all of those aspects of life that prove messy—the cycles of the moon as they cause tides and menses, the changing of seasons with births and deaths—but are requisite for life to continue, weave in relationship with Wisdom . . . a divine being who is bodied and connected."[29] We humans are a *part* of the order of creation, not distinct from it as we believe and too often behave as if we are. Woman Wisdom invites us to reflect on our

---

29. Laura Hobgood-Oster, "Wisdom Literature and Ecofeminism," in *The Earth Story in Wisdom Traditions*, ed. Norman C. Habel and Shirley Wurst, The Earth Bible 3 (Sheffield: Sheffield Academic Press, 2001), 42.

connectedness with God's cosmos. She beckons us to observe God at work
in nature's cycles and seasons.

Jackson's *Wisdom Woman*, along with other illuminations celebrating
Wisdom in *The Saint John's Bible*, draws a strong connection between Wisdom and care for creation. Woman Wisdom invites and aids us to see the
majesty of creation. Indeed, she "emphatically states that she takes delight
in God's creation."[30] Suzanne Moore's abstract patterns in *Praise of Wisdom*
(Sir 24:1-34) invite viewers to see many different natural phenomena—birds,
plants, and fruits—evoking the delightful dance of Wisdom through creation. Moore's bright circular half-moons again emphasize Wisdom's lunar
cycle. Jackson's carpet page for Sirach 51 reminds us that Woman Wisdom
is also a "tree of life" (Prov 3:18).

If we read Hazel Dolby's *Woman of Valor* (Prov 31:10-31) as a poem about
Woman Wisdom, then she becomes not only a co-architect of creation but its
ongoing caretaker. As Michael Patella writes, "God as the Wisdom Woman
of Valor is now presented as the good homemaker, for we encounter God
in the home. . . . Setting up a good household is the symbol for creation
and the world of human habitation."[31] Woman Wisdom's house (Prov 9:1-
6) is thus the entire cosmos. We are to tend to our cosmic home the same
way we would take care of a family home for the next generation. Earth is
not a disposable consumer good. We only hold it in trust for our children,
their children, and all other species with whom they will share the planet.

The close connection between Woman Wisdom and care for creation
evokes Christian ecofeminism. Ecofeminists argue that the human dominance and exploitation of nature is linked to the patriarchal dominance and
exploitation of women.[32] In contrast to the idea that God is distant from
material reality, Christian ecofeminists see "the divine as totally immanent
in creation."[33] The divine, here Wisdom, models her "close relationship with
creation and her commitment to justice" for humankind.[34] Another Christian
ecofeminist writes, "Wisdom Woman sees and describes Earth as a wonder
to behold. . . . She is powerful, but in a transformative way. . . . Wisdom

---

30. Bergant, *A New Heaven, a New Earth*, 105.

31. Patella, *Word and Image*, 161.

32. Heather Eaton, "Ecofeminist Contributions to an Ecojustice Hermeneutics," in
Readings from the Perspective of Earth, ed. Norman C. Habel, The Earth Bible 1 (Sheffield,
UK: Sheffield Academic Press, 2000), 54–71; Clifford, *Introducing Feminist Theology*,
chap. 5, "Feminist Perspectives on Ecology."

33. Clifford, *Introducing Feminist Theology*, 233.

34. Ibid., 248.

is impressive indeed and she is a voice for and of Earth."[35] *The Saint John's Bible*'s intertwining of Woman Wisdom and Creation provokes the question of how *we* can be transformed by an awareness of the different hierarchies and relationships of dominance in which we engage. It bids us to remember the marginalized of the world—the women and children—who are disproportionately displaced by environmental degradation. Meditating on the beauty of Wisdom at creation might just move us to heal that suffering.

CHRIST AND CREATION

> Luke 2:1-14: *Birth of Christ*
> John 1:1-18: *Word Made Flesh*
> Acts 1:8 and 13:47: *You Will Be My Witness* and *To the Ends of the Earth*
> Romans 8: *Fulfillment of Creation*

In Christian faith, Jesus is not just another person. He is God Incarnate, the divine Logos, the New Adam; and his believers' baptism is a new birth. *The Saint John's Bible* echoes Christ's re-creation of the *whole* cosmos in four illuminations in Luke, John, Acts, and Romans.

At first glance, Luke's *Birth of Christ* seems to fit typical nativity scene iconography: the trough, the donkey, the sheep, and the ox. But here the ox, traditionally the symbol of Luke the evangelist, comes from a Neolithic cave painting in Lascaux, France. Since oxen were sacrificed in the Jewish temple, the image at Jesus' birth also hints at Jesus becoming the sacrifice at his death. The motif of the cave painting alludes back to the cave paintings in *Creation* and *Garden of Eden*. The cave painting links these works, as material witnesses to the emergence of distinctly human creativity, to the birth of Christ as a new moment in salvation history. Jesus' birth is like the creation of humankind, because Jesus is a human unlike any other: God and human.

While *Birth of Christ* hints at Jesus as new creation at his birth, *Word Made Flesh* in John portrays Word becoming flesh against a dramatic cosmic backdrop rather than through the intimacy of a baby in a manger. The central figure in this illumination is the bright gold Jesus, seemingly in the middle of being created. To the left of Jesus, Jackson places the text of the hymn in Colossians 1:15-20. Imagery from the Hubble space telescope provides a background, befitting a passage describing Christ in cosmic terms.

35. Hobgood-Oster, "Wisdom Literature and Ecofeminism," 41–42.

Donald Jackson,
John 1:1-18:
Word Made Flesh

The astronomical imagery brings this illumination into conversation with similar imagery in *Creation* and *Wisdom Woman*. Indeed, many of the attributes of Woman Wisdom, such as her presence at creation, are applied to Jesus in the New Testament. While Woman Wisdom is a personification, however, Jesus is a human person. As in *Creation* and *Wisdom Woman*, science expands our understanding of God. The cosmic Christ is visualized as the astronomical Christ. If Christ came to save *all* of creation, that includes other living beings, other planets, even extraterrestrial life. Modern science reminds us that we are only a small piece of God's intergalactic creation. As the Anglican Book of Common Prayer states, "At your command all things came to be: the vast expanse of interstellar space, galaxies, suns, the planets in their courses, and this fragile earth, our island home."[36] Our appreciation of our fragile earth only deepens as we better understand God's universe and our planet's incredibly improbable capacity to sustain life, even as human life now poisons Earth.

By choosing to become enfleshed, God sends a clear message: Flesh is good. Creation is good. Matter matters. *Word Made Flesh* insists on this: " 'Flesh,' in the biblical usage, is not simply what today we name in biological terms as a substance common to animal life and therefore excluding inanimate creation; flesh . . . is that aspect of creation that denotes finitude in contrast to God's eternity."[37] The paradox of the incarnation is that the infinite God becomes finite human, yet it is not a demotion. In *Word Made Flesh*, Jesus' golden body shines brightly, shimmering with divine presence. At the same time, neither here nor in any of his other illuminations does Jackson use stark realism to portray Jesus.[38] Jackson's choice not to give the viewer a detailed portrait of Jesus—short or tall, light- or dark-skinned— lets the viewer imagine for herself the physical form in which Christ might incarnate in her own life.

Word Made Flesh contains the highly stylized text of the Christ hymn in Colossians 1:15-20, presenting a creation-focused scriptural conversation even *within* an illumination. The hymn refers to Jesus as "the image of the invisible God, the firstborn of all creation" (Col 1:15). The first half of this line, "the image of the invisible God," alludes to *Wisdom Woman*, who is also described as the image of God. In *Adam and Eve*, the 2 Corinthians 3:18 marginal quotation reads: "And all of us, with unveiled faces, seeing the glory of the Lord as though reflected in a mirror, are being transformed into the same image from one degree of glory to another." The mirror reveals the image of God, just as Jesus is the image of God. In this conversation between John 1:1-18, Colossians 1:15-20, Wisdom of Solomon 7:22b-30, and 2 Corinthians 3:18, not only is Jesus an image of God, but so is Woman Wisdom, and so are *we* as we draw closer to God through Christ. Like the gold and silver bars of *Wisdom Woman*, the gold of *Word Made Flesh* reflects back

---

36. The Episcopal Church, *Book of Common Prayer* (1979), Eucharistic Prayer C.

37. Mary L. Coloe, "Creation in the Gospel of John," in *Creation Is Groaning: Biblical and Theological Perspectives*, ed. Mary L. Coloe (Collegeville, MN: Michael Glazier, 2013), 87.

38. Jackson's *The Transfiguration* (Mark 9:2-8) is a partial exception, but even there Jesus' face is snow-white, not lifelike. I am indebted to Jason Paul Engel for this point.

to the viewers their own Christlike nature.[39] To top it off: all of this playful discussion about images and mirrors is in a Bible with images.

To return to the second half of Colossians 1:15, Jesus as "the firstborn of all creation" brings us back to Christ as the New Adam. The hymn continues by describing Jesus as the one in whom "all things in heaven and on earth were created, things visible and invisible, whether thrones or dominions or rulers or powers—all things have been created through him and for him" (Col 1:16). It concludes with the bold statement that "through him God was pleased to reconcile to himself all things, whether on earth or in heaven" (Col 1:20a). God did not just reconcile *humanity* to himself, but *all things*, as Christ, "image of . . . God and firstborn of all creation," is "embracing the entire community of Earth, reconciling all of creation to God."[40] The Colossians hymn is not only included in this illumination but is given its own text treatment later in *Letters and Revelation*.

About this hymn, Pope Francis explains that "the mystery of Christ is at work in a hidden manner in the natural world as a whole" (LS 99). The Colossians hymn's "in him all things in heaven and on earth were created" (Col 1:15) echoes John's "all things came into being through him" (John 1:14), indicating that "Jesus is the creator and sustainer of all forms of life and all of creation."[41] And just as through Christ all "things visible and invisible" were created, modern science has enabled us to see parts of creation that for all of human history beforehand *were* invisible: distant galaxies, the inner workings of cells, the development of a baby inside the womb. All these wonders were created through Christ, who, as the Colossians hymn states, is "the image of the invisible God." Just as God became visible through the incarnation, so the Hubble telescope and the many scientists who developed it are incarnating God's invisible creation into images that the human eye can see.

The cosmic context for Jesus' incarnation continues in two Acts illuminations, reflecting Acts 1:8 and 13:47 but located at the end of the book. In Acts 1:8, the risen Jesus tells his disciples that "you will receive power when the Holy Spirit has come upon you; and you will be my witnesses in Jerusalem, in all Judea and Samaria, and *to the ends of the earth*." In Acts 13:47, Paul and Barnabas quote Isaiah 49:6 in their speech in Antioch: "I

39. I am likewise indebted to Engel on this point.
40. Bergant, *A New Heaven, a New Earth*, 159.
41. Thomas Bushlack, "A New Heaven and a New Earth: Creation in the New Testament," in *Green Discipleship: Catholic Theological Ethics and the Environment*, ed. Tobias L. Winright (Winona, MN: Anselm Academic, 2011), 99.

Donald Jackson, Acts 1:8 and 13:47:
To the Ends of the Earth

have set you to be a light for the Gentiles, so that you may bring salvation *to the ends of the earth*."[42] In the context of the first-century Mediterranean, "the ends of the earth" might have meant Spain to the west, Britain to the north, India to the East, and sub-Saharan Africa to the south. The author of Acts would not have known about Antarctica, East Asia, or the Americas. In the twenty-first century, now we have charted not only our planet's surface but other planets' surfaces as well.

Jackson incorporates our expanded vision of creation into his illuminations. In the left-hand side, he places an image of Blue Marble, the famous photo of earth taken from Apollo 8 in 1968. In the right-hand side, Jackson includes the 1997 Hale-Bopp comet. The whirlwind around the comet evokes *Ecclesiastes Frontispiece* and its contrast with Proverbs' *Pillars of Wisdom*, as well as Suzanne Moore's illuminations of *Ruth the Gleaner* and *Huldah the Prophetess*. As with *Word Made Flesh*, this illumination hints at our expanded context of God's creation and Jesus' reconciliation. It seems that we might find extraterrestrial life any day now. How would we include them in Jesus' saving work?

The cosmic significance of salvation through Christ recurs in *Fulfillment of Creation*, Ingmire's illumination to Romans 8. In this passage, Paul

42. Emphasis added.

speaks of how not only humanity but *all* creation "waits with eager longing for the revealing of the children of God" (Rom 8:19). Paul hopes that "the creation itself will be set free from its bondage to decay and will obtain the freedom of the glory of the children of God" (v. 21), a reference to the curse that God placed on humanity in Genesis 3:17. Romans 8, especially 8:19-23, foregrounds the saving work of Jesus for *all* of creation: "there is no reason why ecological misbehaviour and abuse of the environment, whether on an individual or communal scale, should not be seen as outward manifestations of what [Paul] would recognize as a radical slavery to 'Sin.'"[43]

Thomas Ingmire, Romans 8:
Fulfillment of Creation

Ingmire visualizes Romans 8 using the seven days of creation motif already found in *Creation* and *Creation, Covenant, Shekinah, Kingdom.* A shining star at top right alludes again to astronomical imagery. Circular patterns evoke Ingmire's *Out of the Whirlwind* at the end of Job. He also includes text from Romans 8:35 and 8:38, written in a square script like a computer screen, flanked by binary ones and zeroes and mathematical formulas. The binary numbers suggest a connection between God's creation of everything from nothing, and humanity's creation of complex virtual worlds from next to nothing. We can make virtual realities such as Second Life and World of Warcraft out of nothing but ones and zeros. Ingmire uses binary numbers, born of twentieth-century computing, to help the viewer imagine what God's creation and Christ's renewal might mean today. And he sparkles the margins with random shapes, perhaps the particles of creation.

43. Brendan Byrne, "An Ecological Reading of Rom. 8.19-22: Possibilities and Hesitations," in *Ecological Hermeneutics: Biblical, Historical and Theological Perspectives*, ed. David G. Horrell et al. (London: Bloomsbury T&T Clark, 2010), 91.

A NEW HEAVEN AND A NEW EARTH

Revelation 21:1–22:5: *Vision of the New Jerusalem*
1 Corinthians 13:1-13: *Definition of Love*

We began this chapter with *Creation,* the first illumination in *The Saint John's Bible.* Now we turn to the last: *Vision of the New Jerusalem.*

Revelation is the culmination of the whole project. It is by far the most intertextually illuminated book of this Bible. We have already seen an allusion to this passage in Ingmire's illumination to Job 42, which incorporates the text of Revelation 21:4:

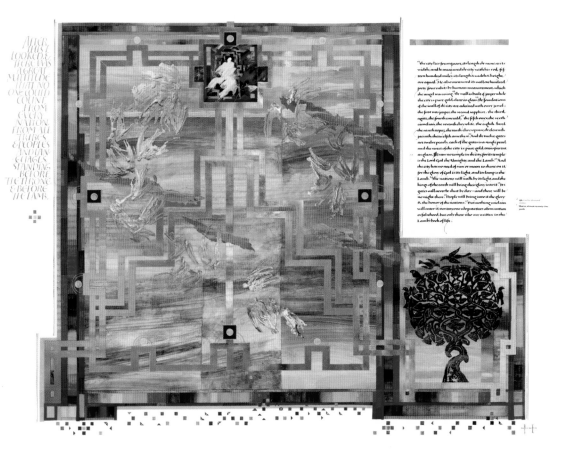

Donald Jackson, Revelation 21:1–22:5: *Vision of the New Jerusalem*

He will wipe every tear from their eyes.
    Death will be no more;
mourning and crying and pain will be no more,
    for the first things have passed away.

Already primed by Job to look ahead to Revelation, we now see the visual fulfillment of the hope of the entire biblical tradition: a new Jerusalem, a new life with God. In *Laudato Si'*, Francis writes, "Even now we are journeying towards the sabbath of eternity, the new Jerusalem, towards our common home in heaven" (LS 243). The illumination envisions the new Jerusalem: lit day and night by the light of God, here the gold leaf; with twelve gates, here twelve pearls reminiscent of the moon cycle in *Wisdom Woman*; led by God enthroned, a motif drawn from the Prophetic Books of *The Saint John's Bible*.

The rainbow border of the image alludes back to *Ecclesiastes Frontispiece*, *Valley of the Dry Bones*, and many other places in *The Saint John's Bible* in which the rainbow appears as a symbol of God's love in never again destroying creation after the Flood. Thomas Ingmire's text treatment of 1 Corinthians 13, the famous "hymn to love," gleams in a bright rainbow pattern. If the rainbow is the quintessential symbol in *The Saint John's Bible* for creation, then this rainbow suggests that love is at the root of all creation, just as love was at the root of God's promise to Noah and to all creation never again to destroy it. If God can flood the entire earth and repopulate it with the help of Noah, then God can bring a heavenly Jerusalem down to earth as well. It is significant that God is not drawing disembodied human souls *up* to a heavenly Jerusalem. God brings Jerusalem *down from* heaven just as Jesus came *down to* humanity in the incarnation: "the earth itself has died . . . the earth is now raised in glory."[44] The rainbow is *the* dominant motif of the book of Revelation, suffusing every illumination in this apex of *The Saint John's Bible*.

The winds in the backdrop of this illumination recall the calm winds in Proverbs' *Pillars of Wisdom*. Likewise, the pearls of the city gates allude to the pearl of wisdom atop one column in *Pillars of Wisdom*. The heavenly Jerusalem *is* the heavenly temple, the house of Wisdom, the most sacred space of spaces. The human author of the book of Revelation was writing decades after Jerusalem was sacked by the Romans and the holy temple burnt to the ground. If God as Creator is proclaimed in his house of Wisdom—in

---

44. Duncan Reid, "Setting aside the Ladder to Heaven: Revelation 21.1–22.5 from the Perspective of the Earth," in *Readings from the Perspective of Earth*, ed. Norman C. Habel, The Earth Bible 1 (Sheffield, UK: Sheffield Academic Press, 2000), 238.

church, temple, abbey, and synagogue—then John of Patmos *sees* God as Creator in his vision of the New Jerusalem. God the Creator is envisioning new life *in this creation*.

Revelation 22:1-5 describes a Tree of Life alongside the river of life running outside the New Jerusalem. This alludes back to the Tree of Life in the Garden of Eden, the tree that is the opposite of the Tree of the Knowledge of Good and Evil from which Eve and Adam ate. Donald Jackson envisions the Tree of Life with one large stamp, which contains twelve fruits on the tree referring back to twelve disciples, twelve tribes of Israel, and other

Thomas Ingmire, 1 Corinthians 13:1-13: *Definition of Love*

significant groups of twelve in the Bible.[45] On the tree are also twelve birds, reminiscent of the ravens in *Creation, Ecclesiastes Frontispiece*, and *Creation, Covenant, Shekinah, Kingdom*.

Finally, the flames in the illumination—perhaps the light of the lamb (Rev 21:23)—allude back to *Creation, Covenant, Shekinah, Kingdom* and its use of fire to evoke the burning bush, and to *Pentecost* and the tongues of fire that helped create the new church. All these flames, elements of creation, create light, light that now suffuses John of Patmos's vision and the colors of this final two-page spread of *The Saint John's Bible*.

Vision of the New Jerusalem brings the viewer-reader of *The Saint John's Bible* back full circle, from cosmic creation with Woman Wisdom, to christological renewal, to eschatological completion. At the end of the Bible, "the radical transformation promised as eschatological fulfillment . . . is actually the force that brings Earth to that fulfillment."[46] Earth is saved along with humanity.

THE CREATION OF *THE SAINT JOHN'S BIBLE*

The incarnation implies that for God, matter *matters*. In Christian faith, God did not just send an abstract message to humankind, but God's *self* as human. Similarly, the process of making the word of God incarnate in *The Saint John's Bible* validates the Bible's materiality. It supplies an illustration of how creation works.

The Saint John's Bible stems from the visions both of the Benedictine tradition of Saint John's Abbey and the modern English calligraphy revival begun by Edward Johnston. Richard Bresnahan works as a potter at Saint John's University. Bresnahan created a kiln on campus, the Johanna kiln—named after his mentor, art historian Johanna Becker, OSB, who also served on the Committee on Illumination and Text. Bresnahan's pottery uses local, organic materials for glazes rather than the usual harmful chemicals.[47] His ethos reflects that of the monastery as a whole, which thinks in long time spans and the deep sustainability of Francis's integral ecology, not in terms of the rapid American economy.

The recovery of the calligraphic arts in England traces its origins to the anti-industrial Arts and Crafts movement of the late nineteenth century.

45. Calderhead, *Illuminating the Word*, 261.
46. Bergant, *A New Heaven, a New Earth*, 182.
47. Calderhead, *Illuminating the Word*, 32–33.

Its largely acknowledged grandfather, Edward Johnston, categorized and taught medieval scripts from his close study of medieval manuscripts and the paleographic research on their letters and scribal techniques.[48] One of Johnston's star pupils, Irene Wellington, went on to have a distinguished teaching career of her own, including one student named Donald Jackson.[49] Trained in this lineage, Jackson is in the minority of calligraphers who still mainly use the old materials.[50] Eschewing the more common metal nib and paper, he prefers the traditional vellum and quill. Some of the professional scribes he hired for the project had little previous experience with these traditional materials.

Jackson's choice of organic physical materials forces him to know intimately his materials and their potential. As Calderhead remarks, "unlike a printed book in which a kind of slick perfection is sought after, a manuscript begins with a material which is organic, variable and has a life of its own. . . . Making the Bible is more like gardening than engineering; it is about working with materials which have personalities of their own."[51] Just as our human minds are imperfect vessels for understanding God's revelation, just as earthly matter is an imperfect medium for expressing God's glory, so Jackson's quills, paint, and vellum are imperfect media for expressing the artistic visions in his mental canvas. His skill as an artist is in his ability to stun despite those limits, precisely *because* of his close relationship with the materiality of his tools and media.

When we look at *The Saint John's Bible*, we must remember its own materiality, the history of its creation. We think of every cow that died for the vellum and every goose whose feathers enabled the vellum to become Scripture. As Aidan Hart remarks, "Painting icons is an ecological act and transfiguring. The iconographer makes the natural materials even more articulate in the praise of God. And all materials have a history that is evoked when you use them. When I paint using eggs from my neighbor's garden I think of the neighbors and the chickens running around."[52] Like Bresnahan, Hart avoids using industrial chemicals from factories. Like Jackson and *The*

48. Donald M. Anderson, *Calligraphy: The Art of Written Forms* (New York: Dover Publications, 1969), 194–96.

49. Rowan Watson, "The Modern Calligraphy Collection of the National Art Library at the Victoria and Albert Museum, London, England," *Calligraphy Review* 5, no. 1 (Fall 1987): 40–45.

50. Calderhead, *Illuminating the Word*, 144.

51. Ibid., 42–43.

52. Ibid., 269.

Saint John's Bible, Hart intends for his sacred art to last for centuries, from his iconostases in Orthodox churches to his smaller icons. Those calves would not give their skin for ephemeral advertisements or political banners. The physicality and sustainability of this Bible's creation corresponds to the care for creation in its illuminations.

CONCLUSION: THE BOOK OF NATURE
AND THE BOOK OF SCRIPTURE

The message and beauty of *The Saint John's Bible* becomes clearer when we look at the way image and image, text and text create a rich conversation. We have seen creation and science, creation and Christ, and creation as a site of God's saving work. In particular, *The Saint John's Bible* connects Wisdom imagery of creation to create an ecofeminist visual exegesis. Woman Wisdom beckons us to follow her wisdom, to nurture creation rather than destroy it.

The Saint John's Bible's ethical imagination beckons specifically for our time in *Valley of the Dry Bones*, visualizing Ezekiel's vision of dead bones being re-enfleshed and resurrected in Ezekiel 37. His vision is a vision of hope: hope that just as God can bring dead bones back to life, so God will bring Israel back to life. The top of this illumination conveys hope through the colors of the rainbow. The bottom of the illumination visualizes what "dry bones" might look like for our time. Jackson drew on images from various twentieth-century genocides in Germany, Malaysia, Bosnia, and elsewhere. Jackson wants us to remember that God can even bring dead bones back to life, that God can make new life even from immense suffering.

Most importantly for our conversation, one of these "dry bones" is an ecological skeleton: a dead car on the center-left of the illumination. Here the illumination reflects the call to *live* ecological justice found in *Laudato Si'* and other Catholic Church teachings on the environment. With ecofeminists, it reminds us that how we treat our fellow humans and how we treat our fellow species are not unrelated. This Bible invites its viewers and readers to work to stop environmental devastation before our planet becomes as dead as the victims of genocide. By putting the beautiful Book of Nature *into* the Book of Scripture, *The Saint John's Bible* invites us to *live* creation care.

CONCLUSION
The Ethical Imagination in Our Time

Throughout this study, we have shown how *The Saint John's Bible* creates canonical conversations that illuminate the ethical-sacramental imaginations of its readers and viewers. *The Saint John's Bible* is not just a beautiful work of art. It is not just an experiment in reviving medieval techniques of bookmaking and calligraphy on a scale unseen in centuries. It is also an invitation to read the Bible with a heart for social justice. Such "beautiful persuasion" does not merely push an agenda on its viewers. Were this art overtly pedantic, it would not be beautiful. Instead, *The Saint John's Bible* suggests connections that fuel the reader-viewer's imagination, empowering one's own voice of conscience.

While we have focused on three broad ethical challenges, several illuminations of *The Saint John's Bible* allude to specific historical events in our time. We have already examined the allusions to twentieth-century genocides in *Valley of the Dry Bones* and the references to the transatlantic slave trade and the prisoners at Guantanamo Bay in *Suffering Servant*. Two more illuminations, however, remind us of the issues of our time to which we must apply our ethical imaginations.

LUKE ANTHOLOGY

Jackson layers the parables in *Luke Anthology* in diagonal columns all pointing to the golden figure of Jesus on the top right—reminding the reader that these parables illustrate the self-sacrificing love of neighbor that Jesus taught. In the column illustrating the parable of the prodigal son (Luke 15:11-32), Jackson includes an allusion to the twin towers destroyed on September 11, 2001.

Donald Jackson, Luke 10; 15; 16:
Luke Anthology, twin towers detail

Jackson was working on this illumination on that day, and saw a connection between the father's forgiveness in the parable and the importance of forgiveness for America in the wake of the traumatic attack.[1] In an interview, Jackson explained that at the time, he hoped to communicate that "Hard as it is, you've got to love your way out of this one[,] you can't hate your way out of it."[2] It is not surprising that Jackson would focus on forgiveness in this parable. Surely it took courage for Jackson to make a bold statement about a trauma so recently inflicted.

FOUR HORSEMEN OF THE APOCALYPSE

John of Patmos's visions of apocalyptic destruction have inspired Christian artists for centuries. It is little wonder, then, that Revelation is one of the most richly illuminated, densely intertextual books of *The Saint John's Bible*.[3] Jackson illuminates the four horsemen of the apocalypse (6:1-8) with four contemporary horrors.

In the text, the four horsemen bring conquest, war, famine, and pestilence and death. Jackson translates these into visual symbols more resonant with our time: oil rigs, tanks, streptococcus bacteria, and nuclear reactor symbols. Jackson was completing these final pages of *The Saint John's Bible* in 2011 as an earthquake struck Japan, creating a nuclear disaster at Fukushima.[4] In this and all other Revelation illuminations, Jackson inserts rainbow imagery as a reminder: despite the obliteration, God has promised not to wholly destroy the world. As in *Valley of the Dry Bones*, God is present even in the horrors—here horrors we enact on each other and on our earth.[5]

---

1. Patella, *Word and Image*, 253.

2. Ileana Llorens, "St. John's Bible Features Hand-Drawn Images, Calligraphy; Apostles Edition to Be Gifted to the Morgan Library and Museum," *Huffington Post*, October 19, 2011, https://www.huffingtonpost.com/2011/10/19/illuminated-st-johns-bible _n_1019800.html.

3. Ibid., 254.

4. Sink, *The Art of* The Saint John's Bible, 322.

5. On this illumination, see also Micah D. Kiel, *Apocalyptic Ecology: The Book of Revelation, the Earth, and the Future* (Collegeville, MN: Liturgical Press, 2017), 106–9.

THE TREE OF LIFE

We have used trees as our guiding symbolic thread throughout *The Saint John's Bible*: the menorah as family tree of Jesus, the olive tree of peace uniting Jews and Christians, the Tree of Knowledge of Good and Evil and the Tree of Life, and the many *actual* trees in our own backyards and parks that nourish all life on earth. The interconnected circles from the Tree of Life in the Sirach 51 carpet page appear in the inner bindings of every volume of the Heritage Edition of *The Saint John's Bible*. The entire Bible, especially this Bible, is a gift of Woman Wisdom, a Tree of Life inviting us to "eat its choicest fruits" (Song 4:16). This tree includes Jews and Christians, Woman Wisdom and Jesus, and our whole ecology. Now this tree beckons you, the reader, to consume its fruits, to chew on them as one chews the cud of the wisdom of Scripture. This *lectio divina* and *visio divina* should not result in contemplation and imagination alone but in action as well. Now the real work begins as you, the reader and viewer, apply the ethical imagination of *The Saint John's Bible* to your own context.

Donald Jackson, Revelation 6:1-8: *Four Horsemen of the Apocalypse*

BIBLIOGRAPHY

Alexander, Loveday C. "Sisters in Adversity: Retelling Martha's Story." In *A Feminist Companion to Luke*, edited by Amy-Jill Levine and Marianne Blickenstaff, 197–213. Cleveland, OH: Pilgrim Press, 2001.

Anderson, Donald M. *Calligraphy: The Art of Written Forms*. New York: Dover Publications, 1969.

Araujo-Hawkins, Dawn. "Q & A with Sr. Glynis Mary McManamon, Moving People through Art." *Global Sisters Report*, June 23, 2016. http://globalsistersreport .org/blog/q/ministry/q-sr-glynis-mary-mcmanamon-moving-people-through -art-40536.

Bellis, Alice Ogden. *Helpmates, Harlots, and Heroes: Women's Stories in the Hebrew Bible*. 2nd ed. Louisville, KY: Westminster John Knox, 2007.

Benedict XVI. "If You Want to Cultivate Peace, Protect Creation." Homily presented at the World Day of Peace, Vatican City, January 1, 2010.

Bergant, Dianne. *A New Heaven, A New Earth: The Bible and Catholicity*. Maryknoll, NY: Orbis Books, 2016.

Berlin, Adele, and Marc Zvi Brettler, eds. *The Jewish Study Bible*. 2nd ed. Oxford: Oxford University Press, 2014.

Binz, Stephen J. *Transformed by God's Word: Discovering the Power of Lectio and Visio Divina*. Notre Dame, IN: Ave Maria Press, 2016.

Bishops' Committee for Ecumenical and Interreligious Affairs, United States Conference of Catholic Bishops. *Criteria for the Evaluation of Dramatizations of the Passion*, 1988.

Bookbinder, Judith. "Synagoga and Ecclesia in Our Time: A Transformative Sculptural Statement in Traditional Form." *Studies in Christian-Jewish Relations* 11, no. 1 (2016). doi:10.6017/scjr.v11i1.9499.

Boys, Mary C. *Has God Only One Blessing? Judaism as a Source of Christian Self-Understanding*. New York: Paulist Press, 2000.

Burton, Keith A. "Numbers." *Eerdmans Dictionary of the Bible*. Edited by David Noel Freedman. Grand Rapids, MI: Eerdmans, 2000.

Bushlack, Thomas. "A New Heaven and a New Earth: Creation in the New Testament." In *Green Discipleship: Catholic Theological Ethics and the Environment*, edited by Tobias L. Winright, 93–111. Winona, MN: Anselm Academic, 2011.

Byrne, Brendan. "An Ecological Reading of Rom. 8.19-22: Possibilities and Hesitations." In *Ecological Hermeneutics: Biblical, Historical and Theological Perspectives*, edited by David G. Horrell, Cheryl Hunt, Christopher Southgate, and Francesca Stavrakopoulou, 83–93. London: Bloomsbury T&T Clark, 2010.

Calderhead, Christopher. "Computer Meets Quill: The Making of a Contemporary Manuscript Bible." *Anglican Theological Review* 83, no. 4 (September 2001): 861–68.

———. *Illuminating the Word: The Making of* The Saint John's Bible. 2nd ed. Collegeville, MN: Liturgical Press, 2015.

Carvalho, Corrine L. "The Book of Ezekiel." In *New Collegeville Bible Commentary: Old Testament*, edited by Daniel Durken. Collegeville, MN: Liturgical Press, 2015.

Clifford, Anne M. *Introducing Feminist Theology*. Maryknoll, NY: Orbis Books, 2000.

Cole, Susan, Marian Ronan, and Hal Taussig. *Wisdom's Feast: Sophia in Study and Celebration*. New ed. Kansas City, MO: Sheed & Ward, 1996.

Coloe, Mary L. "Creation in the Gospel of John." In *Creation Is Groaning: Biblical and Theological Perspectives*, edited by Mary L. Coloe, 71–90. Collegeville, MN: Michael Glazier, 2013.

Commission of the Holy See for Religious Relations with the Jews. *"The Gifts and the Calling of God Are Irrevocable" (Rom 11:29): A Reflection on Theological Questions Pertaining to Catholic-Jewish Relations*, December 10, 2015.

———. *We Remember: A Reflection on the Shoah*, 1998.

Crawford, Sidnie White. "Esther." In *Women's Bible Commentary*, edited by Carol A. Newsom, Sharon H. Ringe, and Jacqueline E. Lapsley, 3rd ed., 201–7. Louisville, KY: Westminster John Knox, 2012.

Croy, N. Clayton, and Alice E. Connor. "Mantic Mary? The Virgin Mother as Prophet in Luke 1.26-56 and the Early Church." *Journal for the Study of the New Testament* 34, no. 3 (2012): 254–76.

Cunningham, Philip A. *Seeking Shalom: The Journey to Right Relationship between Catholics and Jews*. Grand Rapids, MI: Eerdmans, 2015.

D'Alleva, Anne. *Methods & Theories of Art History*. 2nd ed. London: Laurence King Publishing, 2012.

Eaton, Heather. "Ecofeminist Contributions to an Ecojustice Hermeneutics." In *Readings from the Perspective of Earth*, edited by Norman C. Habel, 54–71. The Earth Bible 1. Sheffield, UK: Sheffield Academic Press, 2000.

Exum, J. Cheryl. *Plotted, Shot, and Painted: Cultural Representations of Biblical Women*. Journal for the Study of the Old Testament Supplement Series 215. Sheffield, UK: Sheffield Academic Press, 1996.

———. "Toward a Genuine Dialogue between the Bible and Art." In *Congress Volume Helsinki 2010*, edited by Martti Nissinen, 473–504. Supplements to Vetus Testamentum 148. Leiden: Brill, 2012.

Fanucci, Laura Kelly. "Variation on a Theme: Intertextuality in the Illuminations of the Gospel of Luke." *Obsculta* 2, no. 1 (2009): 21–30.

Felch, Susan. "Reading and Re-Reading the Story of Martha and Mary." Paper presented at Midwest Conference on Christianity and Literature, Spring Arbor University, Spring Arbor, MI, February 19–20, 2016.

Ferguson, George. *Signs and Symbols in Christian Art*. London: Oxford University Press, 1961.

Ferraro, Cari. "Goddess in the Bible." *Alphabet* 34, no. 3 (Summer 2009): 20–25.

Fine, Steven. *The Menorah: From the Bible to Modern Israel*. Cambridge, MA: Harvard University Press, 2016.

Flynn, William. "*In Persona Mariae*: Singing the Song of Songs as a Passion Commentary." In *Perspectives on the Passion: Encountering the Bible through the Arts*, edited by Christine Joynes and Nancy Macky, 106–21. London: Bloomsbury T&T Clark, 2008.

Fraher, Lawrence. "The Illuminated Imagination: Layered Metaphor in *The Saint John's Bible* Frontispiece *Genealogy of Christ*." Unpublished manuscript, May 2, 2014.

Francis (Pope). *Evangelii Gaudium*: Apostolic Exhortation on the Proclamation of the Gospel in Today's World. Vatican City: Liberia Editrice Vaticana, November 24, 2013.

———. *Laudato Si'*: On Care for Our Common Home. Vatican City: Liberia Editrice Vaticana, May 24, 2015.

Frankel, Ellen, and Betsy Platkin Teutsch. *The Encyclopedia of Jewish Symbols*. Northvale, NJ: Jason Aronson, 1995.

Gimbutas, Marija. *The Civilization of the Goddess: The World of Old Europe*. Edited by Joan Marler. New York: HarperCollins, 1991.

———. *The Living Goddesses*. Edited by Miriam Robbins Dexter. Berkeley: University of California Press, 2001.

Gray, Tim. *Praying Scripture for a Change: An Introduction to Lectio Divina*. West Chester, PA: Ascension Press, 2009.

Greeley, Andrew. *The Catholic Imagination*. Berkeley: University of California Press, 2001.

Habel, Norman C. "Geophany: The Earth Story in Genesis 1." In *The Earth Story in Genesis*, edited by Norman C. Habel and Shirley Wurst, 34–48. The Earth Bible 2. Sheffield: Sheffield Academic Press, 2000.

Harrington, Daniel J. *How Do Catholics Read the Bible?* Lanham, MD: Rowman & Littlefield, 2005.

Hengel, Martin. "The Effective History of Isaiah 53 in the Pre-Christian Period." In *The Suffering Servant: Isaiah 53 in Jewish and Christian Sources*, edited by Bernd Janowski and Peter Stuhlmacher, translated by Daniel P. Bailey, 75–146. Grand Rapids, MI: Eerdmans, 2004.

Himes, Michael. "Finding God in All Things: A Sacramental Worldview and Its Effects." In *Becoming Beholders: Cultivating Sacramental Imagination and Actions in College Classrooms*, edited by Karen E. Eifler and Thomas M. Landy. Collegeville, MN: Michael Glazier, 2014.

Hobgood-Oster, Laura. "Wisdom Literature and Ecofeminism." In *The Earth Story in Wisdom Traditions*, edited by Norman C. Habel and Shirley Wurst, 35–47. The Earth Bible 3. Sheffield: Sheffield Academic Press, 2001.

Howard, Cameron B. R. "1 and 2 Kings." In *Women's Bible Commentary*, edited by Carol A. Newsom, Sharon H. Ringe, and Jacqueline E. Lapsley, 3rd ed., 164–79. Louisville, KY: Westminster John Knox, 2012.

Jackson, Donald. "Donald Jackson, Calligrapher." Lecture presented at the EG Conference, Monterey, CA, April 12, 2012. https://vimeo.com/74350010.

———. "The Dream and the Realities." *The Scribe: Journal of the Society of Scribes and Illuminators* 75 (Summer 2002): 3–20.

Janowski, Bernd, and Peter Stuhlmacher, eds. *The Suffering Servant: Isaiah 53 in Jewish and Christian Sources*. Translated by Daniel P. Bailey. Grand Rapids, MI: Eerdmans, 2004.

John Paul II. "Address at the Great Synagogue of Rome." Homily, Great Synagogue of Rome, April 13, 1986. http://www.nytimes.com/1986/04/14/world/text-of -pope-s-speech-at-rome-synagogue-you-are-our-elder-brothers.html.

———. "Address at the Synagogue of Mainz." Homily, Mainz, Germany, November 17, 1980.

Johnson, Luke Timothy, and William S. Kurz. *The Future of Catholic Biblical Scholarship: A Constructive Conversation*. Grand Rapids, MI: Eerdmans, 2002.

Juilfs, Jonathan. "Medieval Apocalypse Books and *The St John's Bible* Book of Revelation." Paper presented at Midwest Conference on Christianity and Literature, Spring Arbor University, Spring Arbor, MI, February 19–20, 2016.

Kiel, Micah D. *Apocalyptic Ecology: The Book of Revelation, the Earth, and the Future*. Collegeville, MN: Liturgical Press, 2017.

Kim, Grace Ji-Sun. "Made in the Image of God: Art, Feminist Theology and Caroline Mackenzie." *Huffington Post*, March 7, 2015. http://www.huffingtonpost.com /grace-jisun-kim/made-in-the-image-of-god-_1_b_6807964.html.

Lee, Dorothy A. "The Heavenly Woman and the Dragon: Rereadings of Revelation 12." In *Feminist Poetics of the Sacred: Creative Suspicions*, edited by Frances Devlin-Glass and Lyn McCredden, 198–220. American Academy of Religion Cultural Criticism Series. Oxford: Oxford University Press, 2001.

Levine, Amy-Jill. "Gospel of Matthew." In *Women's Bible Commentary*, edited by Carol A. Newsom, Sharon H. Ringe, and Jacqueline E. Lapsley, 3rd ed., 465–77. Louisville, KY: Westminster John Knox, 2012.

———. "The Jewish People and Their Sacred Scriptures in the Bible." Lecture, Creighton University, November 2, 2014. https://www.youtube.com/watch?v=C_I8gw9ww5w.

Levine, Amy-Jill, and Marc Zvi Brettler, eds. *The Jewish Annotated New Testament*. Oxford: Oxford University Press, 2011.

Llorens, Ileana. "St. John's Bible Features Hand-Drawn Images, Calligraphy; Apostles Edition to be Gifted to the Morgan Library and Museum." *Huffington Post*, October 19, 2011. https://www.huffingtonpost.com/2011/10/19/illuminated -st-johns-bible_n_1019800.html.

Mackenzie, Caroline. "Intro." *Caroline Mackenzie*. http://carolinemackenzie.co.uk /creative-women/.

Maloney, Linda. "'Swept Under the Rug': Feminist Hermeneutical Reflections on the Parable of the Lost Coin (Lk. 15.8–9)." In *The Lost Coin: Parables of Women, Work, and Wisdom*, edited by Mary Ann Beavis, 34–38. The Biblical Seminar 86. London: Sheffield Academic Press, 2002.

McKibben, Bill. *The Comforting Whirlwind: God, Job, and the Scale of Creation*. Cambridge, MA: Cowley Publications, 2005.

McMahon, Christopher. "Image and Narrative: Reflections on the Theological Significance of *The Saint John's Bible*." *American Benedictine Review* 58, no. 1 (2007): 29–39.

Meyers, Carol. *Rediscovering Eve: Ancient Israelite Women in Context*. Oxford: Oxford University Press, 2012.

Miller, G. D. "Intertextuality in Old Testament Research." *Currents in Biblical Research* 9, no. 3 (2011): 283–309.

Mitchell, Joni. "Big Yellow Taxi," *Ladies of the Canyon*. Los Angeles: A&M Records, 1970.

Murphy, Roland E. *The Tree of Life: An Exploration of Biblical Wisdom Literature*. Grand Rapids, MI: Eerdmans, 2002.

Nanos, Mark D. "Paul and Judaism." In *The Jewish Annotated New Testament*, 551–54. Oxford: Oxford University Press, 2011.

National Conference of Catholic Bishops. *Within Context: Guidelines for the Catechetical Presentation of Jews and Judaism in the New Testament*, 1986.

Niditch, Susan. "Genesis." In *Women's Bible Commentary*, edited by Carol A. Newsom, Sharon H. Ringe, and Jacqueline E. Lapsley, 3rd ed., 27–45. Louisville, KY: Westminster John Knox, 2012.

Nowell, Irene. *Women in the Old Testament*. Collegeville, MN: Liturgical Press, 1997.

Nygard, Travis. "Beautiful Persuasion in Christian Texts: An Analysis of Imagery in the *Moralized Ovid* and *Saint John's Bible* Manuscripts." Paper presented at Midwest Conference on Christianity and Literature, Spring Arbor University, Spring Arbor, MI, February 19–20, 2016.

O'Connor, Kathleen M. "Wild, Raging Creativity: Job in the Whirlwind." In *Earth, Wind, and Fire: Biblical and Theological Perspectives on Creation*, edited by Carol J. Dempsey and Mary Margaret Pazdan, 48–56. Collegeville, MN: Michael Glazier, 2004.

O'Day, Gail R. "Gospel of John." In *Women's Bible Commentary*, edited by Carol A. Newsom, Sharon H. Ringe, and Jacqueline E. Lapsley, 3rd ed., 517–30. Louisville, KY: Westminster John Knox, 2012.

Oegema, Gerbern S. *History of the Shield of David: The Birth of a Symbol*. Frankfurt: Lang, 1996.

———. "The Uses of the Shield of David. On Heraldic Seals and Flags, on Bible Manuscripts, Printer's Marks and Ex Libris." *Jewish Studies Quarterly* 5, no. 3 (1998): 241–53.

Patella, Michael. "Looking into the Bible." In *Becoming Beholders: Cultivating Sacramental Imagination and Actions in College Classrooms*, edited by Karen E. Eifler and Thomas M. Landy. Collegeville, MN: Michael Glazier, 2014.

———. *Word and Image: The Hermeneutics of* The Saint John's Bible. Collegeville, MN: Liturgical Press, 2013.

Pludwinski, Izzy. Interview for *The Saint John's Bible*. YouTube, posted August 21, 2013. https://www.youtube.com/watch?v=ExyyDX_uH4U.

Pontifical Biblical Commission. "Can Women Be Priests?" *Origins* 6 (July 1, 1976), 92-96.

———. *The Interpretation of the Bible in the Church*. Vatican City: Libreria Editrice Vaticana, 1993.

———. *The Jewish People and Their Sacred Scriptures in the Christian Bible*. Vatican City: Libreria Editrice Vaticana, 2002.

Reid, Barbara E. *Choosing the Better Part? Women in the Gospel of Luke*. Collegeville, MN: Michael Glazier, 1996.

———. "The Gospel According to Matthew." In *New Collegeville Bible Commentary: New Testament*, edited by Daniel Durken, 1–90. Collegeville, MN: Liturgical Press, 2009.

———. *Wisdom's Feast: An Invitation to Feminist Interpretation of the Scriptures*. Grand Rapids, MI: Eerdmans, 2016.

Reid, Duncan. "Setting aside the Ladder to Heaven: Revelation 21.1–22.5 from the Perspective of the Earth." In *Readings from the Perspective of Earth*, edited by Norman C. Habel, 232–45. The Earth Bible 1. Sheffield, UK: Sheffield Academic Press, 2000.

Renfro, Kyndall. "Faithful Disciple, Feminine Witness: Mary Magdalene Revisited." *Review & Expositor* 110, no. 1 (2013): 131–36.

Schaberg, Jane D., and Sharon H. Ringe. "Gospel of Luke." In *Women's Bible Commentary*, edited by Carol A. Newsom, Sharon H. Ringe, and Jacqueline E. Lapsley, 3rd ed., 493–511. Louisville, KY: Westminster John Knox, 2012.

Scholem, Gershom. "The Star of David: History of a Symbol." In *The Messianic Idea in Judaism and Other Essays on Jewish Spirituality*, 257–81. New York: Schocken, 1971.

Schüssler Fiorenza, Elisabeth. *Wisdom Ways: Introducing Feminist Biblical Interpretation*. Maryknoll, NY: Orbis Books, 2001.

Sink, Susan. *The Art of* The Saint John's Bible: *The Complete Reader's Guide*. Collegeville, MN: Liturgical Press, 2013.

Sinnott, Alice M. "Job 12: Cosmic Devastation and Social Turmoil." In *The Earth Story in Wisdom Traditions*, edited by Norman C. Habel and Shirley Wurst, 78–91. The Earth Bible 3. Sheffield: Sheffield Academic Press, 2001.

Smith, Mark S. "The Book of Exodus." In *New Collegeville Bible Commentary: Old Testament*, edited by Daniel Durken. Collegeville, MN: Liturgical Press, 2015.

Song, Angeline. "Heartless Bimbo or Subversive Role Model? A Narrative (Self) Critical Reading of the Character of Esther." *Dialog* 49, no. 1 (2010): 56–69.

Steffler, Alva William. *Symbols of the Christian Faith*. Grand Rapids, MI: Eerdmans, 2002.

Stewart, Anne W. "Deborah, Jael, and Their Interpreters." In *Women's Bible Commentary*, edited by Carol A. Newsom, Sharon H. Ringe, and Jacqueline E. Lapsley, 3rd ed., 128–32. Louisville, KY: Westminster John Knox, 2012.

Tull, Patricia K. "Rhetorical Criticism and Intertextuality." In *To Each Its Own Meaning: An Introduction to Biblical Criticisms and Their Application*, edited by Steven L. McKenzie and Stephen R. Haynes, rev. ed., 156–79. Louisville, KY: Westminster John Knox, 1999.

United States Conference of Catholic Bishops. *Renewing the Earth: An Invitation to Reflection and Action on Environment in Light of Catholic Social Teaching*, November 14, 1991.

Vatican Council II: Constitutions, Decrees, Declarations; The Basic Sixteen Documents. Edited by Austin Flannery. Collegeville, MN: Liturgical Press, 2014.

Watson, Rowan. "The Modern Calligraphy Collection of the National Art Library at the Victoria and Albert Museum, London, England." *Calligraphy Review* 5, no. 1 (Fall 1987): 40–45.

Wilson, Brittany E. "Mary Magdalene and Her Interpreters." In *Women's Bible Commentary*, edited by Carol A. Newsom, Sharon H. Ringe, and Jacqueline E. Lapsley, 3rd ed., 531–35. Louisville, KY: Westminster John Knox, 2012.

Witherington, Ben, III. *Isaiah Old and New: Exegesis, Intertextuality, and Hermeneutics*. Minneapolis, MN: Fortress Press, 2017.

Wurst, Shirley. "Woman Wisdom's Way: Ecokinship." In *The Earth Story in Wisdom Traditions*, edited by Norman C. Habel and Shirley Wurst, 48–64. The Earth Bible 3. Sheffield: Sheffield Academic Press, 2001.

Yarden, Leon. *The Tree of Light: A Study of the Menorah, The Seven-Branched Lampstand*. Ithaca, NY: Cornell University Press, 1971.

Yoder, Christine Roy. "Proverbs." In *Women's Bible Commentary*, edited by Carol A. Newsom, Sharon H. Ringe, and Jacqueline E. Lapsley, 3rd ed., 232–42. Louisville, KY: Westminster John Knox, 2012.

SCRIPTURE INDEX

ILLUMINATION INDEX

MARGINALIA AND DECORATIONS